American Kasten

◆

American Kasten

◆

The Dutch-Style Cupboards of New York and New Jersey 1650–1800

◆

PETER M. KENNY

FRANCES GRUBER SAFFORD

GILBERT T. VINCENT

The Metropolitan Museum of Art

New York

This catalogue is published in conjunction with the exhibition
American Kasten: The Dutch-Style Cupboards of New York and New Jersey, 1650–1800
held at The Metropolitan Museum of Art, New York,
January 19–April 7, 1991.

This publication has been made possible by support from
The Chipstone Foundation, Dr. and Mrs. John J. Weber,
The William Cullen Bryant Fellows, Israel Sack, Inc.,
The Wunsch Foundation, and the Shawangunk Valley Conservancy.

Published by The Metropolitan Museum of Art, New York

John P. O'Neill, Editor in Chief
Barbara Burn, Executive Editor
Ruth Lurie Kozodoy, Editor
Margaret Davis, Design and Typography
Susan Chun, Production

Printed by Colorcraft Lithographers, Inc., New York
Bound by Sendor Bindery, New York

Library of Congress Cataloging-in-Publication Data

Kenny, Peter M.
American kasten : the Dutch-style cupboards of New York and New Jersey, 1650–1800 / by Peter M. Kenny, Frances Gruber Safford, and Gilbert T. Vincent
p. cm.
Includes bibliographical references.
ISBN 0-87099-605-3 (pbk.)
1. Cupboards—New York (State)—History—17th century—Exhibitions. 2. Cupboards—New York (State)—History—18th century—Exhibitions. 3. Furniture, Dutch colonial—New York (State)—Exhibitions. 4. Furniture, Baroque—New York (State)—Exhibitions. 5. Cupboards—New Jersey—History—17th century—Exhibitions. 6. Cupboards—New Jersey—History—18th century—Exhibitions. 7. Furniture, Dutch colonial—New Jersey—Exhibitions. 8. Furniture, Baroque—New Jersey—Exhibitions. I. Safford, Frances Gruber. II. Vincent, Gilbert Tapley, 1946– . III. Metropolitan Museum of Art (New York, N.Y.) IV. Title. NK2727.K46 1991
749'.3—dc20 90-24963
CIP

Photographs were provided courtesy of the institutions credited except for catalogue numbers 1, 6, 7, 9, 10, 11, 12, 13, 14, 16, 17, and figures 14, 15, 21, 22, 23, 25, 31, 38, 39, 40, 41, 42, which were taken by Jerry Thompson, and figure 16, taken by Luigi Pellettieri. The line drawings are by Daniel Hopping. The map was drawn by Wilhelmina T. Reyinga-Amrhein.

Front cover: Kast, catalogue number 9
Back cover: Details, cornices of kasten, catalogue numbers 9 and 3
Title-page spread: Kast, catalogue number 8

Contents

◆

Foreword

◆

More than half a century has passed since any exhibition at the Metropolitan Museum has focused on furniture made in our own region. The first major exploration of the subject as a whole, *A Loan Exhibition of New York State Furniture*, included items from the seventeenth through the mid-nineteenth century. It was organized by Joseph Downs in 1934, the year he became curator of the American Wing, which had just been formed to serve as a separate department for American decorative arts. That exhibition presented pieces that were distinctive New York interpretations of English-derived colonial styles and also showed furniture that clearly reflected the Dutch cultural heritage of the colony. Chief among the latter were large cupboards called *kasten*, examples of a furniture form recognized since the beginning of the century as quintessentially Dutch in inspiration. Two kasten were in the exhibition: the grisaille-painted kast now at the Van Cortlandt House in the Bronx and the gumwood one that is number six in this catalogue. Now, decades later, this imposing furniture form is carefully examined in the present catalogue and the exhibition it accompanies.

It happens that the first example of New York colonial furniture to enter the collections of this Museum was a kast with striking grisaille decoration that depicts large pendants of fruit in niches (number 5 in this catalogue). It was purchased in 1909, the year that the Museum also acquired as a gift from Mrs. Russell Sage the large H. Eugene Bolles collection of early New England furniture. With the 1918 purchase of a select group of late-colonial furniture from Bolles's cousin and fellow-collector George S. Palmer a solid nucleus for an American furniture collection was formed, but one with a strong New England bias. Through the years, however, individual New York pieces were steadily acquired by gift or by purchase, and the Museum now owns one of the most comprehensive representations of this region's furniture.

A second grisaille-painted kast entered the Museum collections in 1923. It had long been owned by the Hewlett family, whose Long Island house furnished the woodwork that was installed the following year in the American Wing. An important recent addition is a seventeenth-century oak kast with a marbleized surface (catalogue number 3) which becomes the collections' sole representative of joined oak furniture from New York. The kast, known to Downs but not included in the 1934 exhibition, had been lost from view until three years ago, when it was offered as a gift just as preparations for this exhibition were getting underway.

The exhibition *American Kasten: The Dutch-Style Cupboards of New York and New Jersey, 1650–1800* and its catalogue result from the joint ideas and efforts of Frances Gruber Safford, Associate Curator of American Decorative Arts, Peter M. Kenny, Assistant Curator of American Decorative Arts, and Gilbert T. Vincent, an independent curator and specialist in the area of New York decorative arts, who began working together on the project as early as 1986. However, no exhibition can take place without financial support, and the generous underwriting provided by The Chipstone Foundation, Dr. and Mrs. John J. Weber, The William Cullen Bryant Fellows, Israel Sack, Inc., The Wunsch Foundation, and the Shawangunk Valley Conservancy has made the exhibition and especially its accompanying publication possible. We are deeply grateful for their sponsorship and their thoughtful encouragement.

John K. Howat
The Lawrence A. Fleischman Chairman
of the Departments of American Art

Introduction

◆

Studying the American Kast

This examination of the American kast is intended to fill a sizable gap in the study of American furniture. Hardly any scholarly work has been done on kasten. Seventeenth-century joined oak furniture from the New York area is virtually unknown; the four rare examples discussed here should provide a welcome point of comparison with better-known case furniture from New England. While the later Baroque-style kasten from the New York area are more familiar, these distinctive case pieces, too, despite the fact that they number well into the hundreds, have not been comprehensively studied. Additionally, the names of only two makers are known to date, examples from Connecticut have never been discussed, and a viable chronology and analyses of regional characteristics have been published only piecemeal. Confusion exists even over the terminology applied to this distinctive furniture form, a subject that deserves to be addressed first.

After the conquest of New Netherland by an English fleet in 1664 (except for the brief period of Dutch reconquest in 1673–74), English was the mandated language of government documents. Thus, most contemporary wills and inventories, which were an English legality, use the term "cupboard," or a phonetic equivalent such as "cubbert." In English, cupboard is a generic term for any wooden case piece with doors. Cupboards came in all shapes and sizes and served a variety of purposes, from storing clothes, textiles, and food to displaying valuable silver and ceramics, but distinctions of function were rarely made in inventories and wills.

From time to time, in inventories from the Dutch-speaking hinterlands well beyond the seat of English colonial government in New York City, local parlance creeps in and clarifies matters. Two examples from Albany verify the use of the word "cupboard" to designate the kast. In 1739 Elsie Egbertse asked that her brother receive her "cupboard (or in Dutch Cass)."[1] In 1753 Isaac Fryor left his daughter his "Great Cupboard or Kass."[2] A third example illustrates another English variant spelling of kast. Theunis Van Vechten of Catskill, New York, bequeathed to his wife "the use but not the disposing of my large Cupboard or in Dutch called 'Groote Case.'"[3]

The words "kas" and "kast" were used interchangeably in seventeenth- and eighteenth-century American inventories, and the Dutch terminology may have survived through the nineteenth century among some colonial families of New York and New Jersey. The term "kas" was reintroduced to the general public by the earliest historians of American furniture, particularly Esther Singleton, at the beginning of the present century,[4] and has become commonly accepted in the field. However, in this study the word "kast" and the plural "kasten" will be used, since these words were employed in colonial America and are also the current Dutch terms. This makes the American term identical with its Dutch counterpart and eliminates the need for English mutations such as "kases."

In another question of terminology, the decision was made to call the style of eighteenth-century kasten "Baroque" rather than "William and Mary," a name that has been applied to the form in the past. "Baroque," the term used by Dutch historians of furniture, avoids connotations of Englishness and emphasizes the Dutch origins of this particular American form.

The kast has been recognized as a feature of colonial New York furniture since the first formal studies in this field. In 1900 Singleton identified as kasten documented examples still in the possession of New York Dutch families[5] and cited references from many colonial inventories and wills. However, she illustrated only European-made kasten. The following year Luke Vincent Lockwood reaffirmed the connection between kasten and areas of Dutch culture in America. He published the first illustrations of American kasten, showing the grisaille-painted example (which he misidentified as Dutch) now at the Frederick Van Cortlandt House in the Bronx, and one from Connecticut described as being made of maple.[6]

The standard design of pure Dutch origin had been recognized by 1902, when Frances Clary Morse wrote that the American kast "was usually made in two parts, the upper one having two doors and a heavy cornice above. The lower part held a long drawer and rested upon large ball feet."[7] The earlier oak kasten were still unknown, and those combining the Dutch form with a mix of English details were for the most part ignored. Subsequent historians of American furniture have mentioned the kast and its unique role as part of the Dutch heritage of the New York area, but they have provided few new insights. A possible explanation for this seeming indifference and for the fact that few major collections of American furniture include a kast was offered in 1928 by Wallace Nutting, who noted, "The kas has never been popular as an article to collect. This might not be the case if collectors had great rooms and much bare space. As it is, collectors are jealous of their rooms, which are usually overcrowded anyway."[8] The American kast was so little studied that its Baroque features continually inspired incorrect dating.

The first furniture historian to suggest in print the existence of identifiable groups or schools of American kasten was Dean Failey, who illustrated examples from two regions of Long Island.[9] He noted marked differences in design between kasten attributed to Kings County and those from central Long Island, which incorporate English details. The rare but visually impressive grisaille-painted kasten were the first to be studied as an identifiable subgroup, one bound by similarities of decoration rather than construction. In 1980 Patricia Chapin O'Donnell published six examples of this type, attributing four of them to the same painter.[10] Two more examples were identified by Firth Haring Fabend the following year.[11]

In 1986 an extensive exhibition, *Remembrance of Patria: Dutch Arts and Culture in Colonial America, 1609–1776*, was mounted at the Albany Institute of History & Art. A catalogue and the proceedings of a symposium held in conjunction with the exhibition added more examples and further documentation to the history of the American kast.[12] In particular, Roderic Blackburn directed attention to the grisaille-painted kasten and their possible sources in the Netherlands, and Joyce Geary Volk conducted a structural comparison of a kast signed by Roelof Demarest with another example from the Bergen County area.[13]

In the present study, Gilbert T. Vincent discusses the European background of kasten and their role in American domestic life. Frances Gruber Safford analyzes the four known kasten made in the joined oak tradition and also the disparate group decorated with grisaille painting. Peter M. Kenny examines the sizable body of surviving American Baroque kasten and traces several regional schools and local styles. It is hoped that this catalogue and the exhibition that it accompanies will encourage a renewed appreciation for these remarkable pieces of American furniture and thus bring additional kasten and documentation to light.

Notes

1. *Collections of the New-York Historical Society for the Year 1895* (New York, 1896), p. 440.
2. Ibid., p. 87.
3. Quoted in Joseph Downs, *American Furniture: Queen Anne and Chippendale Periods* (New York, 1952), no. 263.
4. Singleton, *Furniture of Our Forefathers*, p. 264.
5. Ibid., pp. 234–311.
6. Luke Vincent Lockwood, *Colonial Furniture in America* (New York, 1901), pp. 96–103.
7. Frances Clary Morse, *Furniture of the Olden Time* (New York, 1902), p. 86.
8. Wallace Nutting, *Furniture Treasury* (Framingham, Mass., 1928), no. 481.
9. Failey, *Long Island Is My Nation*, pp. 109–10.
10. O'Donnell, "Grisaille Decorated *Kasten*," pp. 1108–11.
11. Firth Haring Fabend, "Two 'New' Eighteenth-Century Grisaille Kasten," *Clarion*, Spring/Summer 1981, pp. 44–49.
12. Blackburn and Piwonka, *Remembrance of Patria*; and *New World Dutch Studies*.
13. Roderic H. Blackburn, "Transforming Old World Dutch Culture via New World Environment: Processes of Material Adaptation," in *New World Dutch Studies*, pp. 98–99; and Joyce Geary Volk, "The Dutch Kast and the American Kas: A Structural/Historical Analysis," in *New World Dutch Studies*, pp. 107–17.

American Kasten

◆

Origins and Uses

The American kast is a large, freestanding wooden cupboard or wardrobe, generally with two doors. Inside are two or three widely spaced shelves; the more elaborate pieces have a drawer in the base section for additional storage. In America kasten were made exclusively in the Dutch cultural areas of New York, New Jersey, and Connecticut in the period from the mid-seventeenth century to the first quarter of the nineteenth century. (The kast is not to be confused with the Pennsylvania-German cupboard called a *Schrank*, which has pegs for hanging clothes and is assembled differently.[1])

The earliest surviving American kasten are four multipaneled examples built of joined oak, a type of construction which had characterized Dutch kasten through the first half of the seventeenth century. By 1700 a new design, related in style to Dutch Baroque kasten of the second half of the seventeenth century, had developed in the Dutch settlements in America. This design is distinguished by two large doors, each with a panel and moldings, set between decorative stiles. The top is a massive cornice that angles out at forty-five degrees. The base section contains a long drawer. The whole rests on four feet, the two in front of a voluminous ball design and those in back of inconspicuous board (fig. 1). In simpler versions of this type the base section with its drawer is absent, and the cornice is usually smaller in scale.

1. Kast, Bergen County, New Jersey, 1760–80. Red gum and yellow poplar with paint added later, H. 77 1/2 in. (196.8 cm). Minneapolis Institute of Arts, The Putnam Dana McMillan Fund (81.3)

The eighteenth-century kast of Dutch design is unusual among American furniture forms because it survived essentially unchanged until the early 1800s, through several periods of stylistic innovation. That continuity most likely reflects the relative isolation of the areas of Dutch culture, which were to be found on western and central Long Island, in the Hackensack, Passaic, and Raritan River valleys in New Jersey, and along both sides of the Hudson River from New York City to the Albany area (see map, fig. 2). A similar conservatism, if not of quite the same longevity, has been noted in the design of chairs and in the silver, painting, and architecture of New York State.[2]

The New Netherland colony, founded in 1624, was from the beginning a mixture of ethnic groups and nationalities. A French Jesuit who visited New Amsterdam in 1643 was told by Willem Kieft, director general of the colony, that the inhabitants of the fledgling port spoke "eighteen different languages."[3] This internationalism reflected the unusually tolerant nature of seventeenth-century Dutch society. It has been estimated that only about one half of the New Netherland population was Dutch by birth or heritage;[4] however, most colonists acceded to Dutch cultural dominance, speaking the Dutch language and acknowledging the leadership of the Dutch Reformed Church. Direct contact with the Netherlands was increasingly cut off after the British took over in 1664, but for many settlers of Flemish, French, or German heritage, the Dutch culture was more familiar than the English one. Comfortable with what they knew, they tended to reject changes that came from the outside and sought to preserve much of the past.

This was especially the case with rural inhabitants, most of all the independent small farmers. The

2. Areas of Dutch settlement in America with county boundaries of 1790. Inset: Kings County (now Brooklyn)

countryside had remained untouched by the bloodless English conquest which occurred when the Dutch governor, Peter Stuyvesant, surrendered, after a week's reflection, to an English fleet. While the governing administration changed—for the better, according to many accounts—the individual rights and privileges that had existed under the Dutch continued as before. Securely entrenched on rich farmland and clustered about their Dutch Reformed churches, the country people remained distant from the new government. An export trade that now included commerce with the expanding British empire was making them increasingly prosperous. They were more than content with their daily lives, speaking a Dutch dialect, building farmhouses and barns in a colonial Dutch style, and receiving new ministers sent from the Classis in Amsterdam until well after the American Revolution. The exceptions were those colonists with an interest in commerce or government. They included the large landowners and many of the Dutch merchants in New York City, all of whom found it expedient to protect their livelihood and property by giving support to the English government.

Thus in the late 1740s, eighty-five years after the English conquest, New York was still identifiably Dutch, as the Swedish naturalist Peter Kalm noted: "The inhabitants, both of the town [New York City] and the province belonging to it, are yet for the greater part Dutchmen; who still, especially the old people, speak their mother tongue."[5] The persistence of the Dutch language ultimately became a source of ridicule. The Dutch, many of whom never learned proper English, were called "ignorant" and "boors," a pejorative term derived from *boer*, Dutch for farmer. Although Kalm mentioned a growing acceptance of the English language and culture in New York City, over fifty years later Albany remained disconcertingly Dutch to the educator Timothy Dwight. It was Dutch in "its whole aspect and character"; the buildings were "ordinary, dull and disagreeable" and greatly in need of improvement "in the English manner."[6] Luckily, Dwight

3. Kast, Dutch, dated 1622. Oak, H. 96 in. (243.8 cm). The Metropolitan Museum of Art, Fletcher Fund, 1964 (64.81)

commented, Albany was undergoing transformation thanks to several devastating fires and an influx of New Englanders.

For those inhabitants of New York and New Jersey who valued their Dutch heritage and could afford the expense, the kast was an important material possession. In the few New York wills that list furniture, the kast is often mentioned; among the very few colonial inventories, only expensive items such as the tester bed with all its hangings regularly exceeded the kast in value.

Unlike strongly regional Dutch colonial architecture, which has a different character in each area of settlement, kast design is remarkably consistent. Only minor variations distinguish kasten made in Manhattan and western Long Island, in central and northeastern New Jersey, and in the Hudson River Valley. Yet analysis of the nearly two hundred examples documented to date has shown them to be the handiwork of many different makers working over four or five generations. (Marked differences in design do appear in the border areas of Dutch settlement, where Dutch and English cultures interacted.)

The Dutch Kast

The American kast is but one variant emerging from the large body of cupboard furniture made throughout Europe, beginning with the cupboards built for both sacred and secular use in the medieval church. Particularly in Germany and the Netherlands, the cupboard evolved as one of the principal furniture forms. In the Netherlands there were two basic types of kast: a two-stage, four-door cupboard, the dominant form in the late sixteenth and first half of the seventeenth centuries; and a one-stage cupboard with two doors, which was to become the preferred type after 1650.

Early kasten were built of oak and joined in the same way as the framed paneling found in finer houses of the period. Furniture, however, was more likely than paneling to be embellished with extensive carving and a rich combination of the classically derived ornaments that were disseminated in northern Europe through books of engraved designs, such as the works of Hans Vredeman de Vries (1527–1604). His widely known furniture designs promulgated a lavish surface treatment with an expressive mélange of cornices, bosses, panels, caryatids, columns, niches, and pilasters combined in a dramatic but unclassical proportional mix, a style that has been classified as Mannerist. A typical example of this Mannerist design is a two-stage kast dated 1622, shown in figure 3. The idiosyncratic nature of the style was fully realized at the time: the painter and writer Karel van Mander (1548–1606), who had spent three years in Rome as a student and was knowledgeable about classical architecture, lamented, "This rein is so free and this license so misused by our Netherlanders that in the course of time in building a great heresy has arisen among them, with a heap of craziness of decorations and the breaking of pilasters in the middle, and adding on pedestals, their usual coarse points of diamonds and such lameness, very disgusting to see."[7]

More subdued designs, including plans for one- and two-stage kasten (figs. 4, 5), were published in 1642 by the printmaker Crispin de Passe the Younger (1593–1670). This soberer approach to architecture and decoration marks the beginning of what is now known as seventeenth-century Dutch classicism.[8] The new taste was promoted by Frederik Hendrik, who was stadtholder beginning in 1624. It became the national style of the Netherlands throughout its famed Golden Age. Wealth was flooding into the port cities, the lion's

4, 5. Crispin de Passe the Younger (Dutch, 1593–1670), two engraved designs for kasten. From *Oficina Arcularia* (Amsterdam, 1642), plates F, E. The Metropolitan Museum of Art, Harris Brisbane Dick Fund, 1923 (23.34.1)

share going to Amsterdam, which had succeeded Antwerp as the banking center of northern Europe. Amsterdam was also controlling the Baltic Sea trade, expanding trade rapidly in the Mediterranean area and the East Indies, and building the majority of the renowned Dutch merchant ships.[9] To its prosperous bourgeois, a dignified and worldly expression of their stature seemed better found in a style more academically correct, classical, and closer to the Italian original than the Mannerism of the preceding generations. The new attitude was epitomized by the work of the architect Jacob van Campen (1595–1657), particularly his celebrated masterpiece, the Amsterdam Town Hall, begun in 1648. Its principal facade adornments were simple pilasters and restrained swags (fig. 6). Other architects and builders more or less followed van Campen's lead, and a new architectural classicism arose favoring balance, regularity, and academic details, as exemplified by the interior paneling shown in figure 7.[10]

In kast design, the older two-stage form, its facade broken into many units, gave way, in the period of Dutch classicism, to a one-stage, two-door cupboard with a single panel on each door. Contrasts were sought through the use of different woods, as is illustrated in de Passe's design (fig. 5). At first oak remained the primary wood, and ebony insets enlivened the surface (fig. 10). After about 1650 the form became grander and more opulent, incorporating veneers of exotic woods such as rosewood with contrasts of ebony, applied to oak carcases. This use of rich materials characterized the Baroque phase of Dutch classicism, as did monumental proportions and dramatic extensions and indentations that created a play of movement over the entire facade.

6. Engraving of the Amsterdam Town Hall designed by Jacob van Campen (Dutch, 1595–1657), from a drawing by A. de Putter. In *Architecture, peinture et sculpture de la Maison de Ville d'Amsterdam* (Amsterdam, 1719). In the mid-17th century, few buildings rivaled this structure for size or magnificence.

Especially prominent were the massive door panels, which projected forcefully from the front of the case. In the Netherlands a bold beveled panel of this type became known as a *kussen* (cushion); catalogue number 7 is a *kussenkast* from the second half of the seventeenth century. The overscale cornice, half-round columns, and waved moldings on these kasten further intensify their dynamic effect.

At a later stage the Baroque design moderated: the door panels flattened out, the waved moldings disappeared, and the contrasting woods of the *kussenkast* gave way to an overall veneer of rosewood or walnut. Instead of half columns or panels applied to the stiles, a flat pilaster was consistently used together with applied carving similar to that designed by van Campen and his school (fig. 8).

While the exterior of the Baroque kast proclaimed both material substance, with its size and rich carving, and respectful knowledge of classical antiquity, with its columns, pilasters, and moldings, the interior was purely functional. Its primary and traditional household use was the storage of linen, as documented in Pieter de Hooch's masterpiece *The Linen Closet,* painted in 1663.[11] A housewife and a maid stand before the open doors of an oak kast with ebony insets. The maid holds a stack of cleaned and pressed linen, an empty laundry basket behind her. Instructions in household

7. Woodwork from an Amsterdam interior, Dutch, 1650–75. Oak. Rijksmuseum, Amsterdam

guidebooks of the time advised that linens be stored in the kast; Dutch emblem books—small, inexpensive publications with woodcuts accompanied by moral aphorisms, intended for mass consumption—provide many illustrations of this use. The kasten are shown in interior scenes serving as storage units for textiles and valuables of all sorts, with expensive ceramics, glass, and silver displayed on the tops. (See, additionally, figs. 9, 36.)

Seventeenth- and eighteenth-century social practices required the extensive use of textiles. Yards of hanging fabrics, as well as the usual sheets and pillowcases, covered the beds. Curtains hung in windows, and decorative coverings often enlivened tables and chests. Throughout the seventeenth century, most genteel seating furniture incorporated one or more cushions. Large napkins were necessary at each meal, since people ate with their fingers before the general introduction of forks. Until the late eighteenth century all these textiles were handwoven, and they were expensive. Although the simpler weaving could be done at home, eliminating a direct labor expense, a considerable investment of time was still involved. Women were encouraged to begin at a young age to make and acquire textiles for a dowry. In the Netherlands and areas of Dutch culture these were stored in a kast, if the family could afford one.

The emblem books and household guides—such as *De ervarene en verstandige Hollandsche huyshoudster* (The experienced and knowledgeable Hollands householder)—celebrated the Dutch home as the wellspring and safeguard of the Dutch nation. It fulfilled that function only if it was well ordered, spotlessly clean, and suitably religious; householders were continually advised to maintain high standards. The guides recommended that laundry be washed every day and tablecloths, napkins, pillows, and sheets carefully dried, pressed, and safely stored.[13] Travelers to the Netherlands frequently commented on what struck them as an unnatural obsession with cleanliness. One disgruntled Englishman, complaining about the perilous height of Dutch cabin beds, acknowledged that at least there would be the minor compensation "of having died in clean linen."[14] Frenchmen found the Dutch compulsion for cleanliness equally outlandish.[15]

This distinctive Dutch trait has been explained as the product of a damp climate that promoted mold and mildew and produced an endless supply of mud. However, the Dutch climate does not differ significantly from that of neighboring countries. It is the well-argued thesis of Simon Schama that the Dutch

8. Kast, Dutch, possibly Groningen, dated 1689. Rosewood veneer on oak, H. 89 3/8 in. (227 cm). Rijksmuseum, Amsterdam

penchant for cleanliness arose from more profound needs.[16] The Dutch were hardly a nation when the seven northern provinces declared independence from Spain in 1581. War, often brutal and merciless, absorbed them for the next eighty years, and in addition, much of their land was exposed to destruction by the sea. These experiences intensified the effect of strict Christian precepts in which fear of the deluge was counterbalanced by a concern for salvation. In time, inordinate wealth and power flowed into the Dutch republic, threatening to subvert the redemptive restraint, simplicity, and humility encouraged by the Calvinist church. The orderly house can thus be seen as a symbolic embodiment of the Dutch people for whom constant vigilance was required against defilement and destruction, whether the source was the Spanish, the sea, or the devil.

It is also true that the Dutch inhabited a small territory and that to live in their confined quarters they had to be well organized. The spotless house is probably a manifestation of all these circumstances, both spiritual and pragmatic.

From the Netherlands to America

In America the earliest kasten, despite differences between them, all derive from multipaneled Dutch oak kasten of Mannerist and early classicist style. The American examples are so few in number and their designs so greatly simplified, however, that it is difficult to extrapolate a close relationship.

Later American kasten in the Baroque style present a surprising uniformity. They are made of hardwood and their facades are very similar, even though three quite different methods of construction were variously employed: in one piece as a single unit; in two pieces with the upper part resting on the base; and in three pieces with a detachable cornice (Appendix A). The

9. Jan van der Heyden (Dutch, 1637–1712), Engraving. In *Beschrijving Der nieuwlijks uitgevonden en geoctrojeerde Slang-Brand-Spuiten . . .* (Amsterdam, 1690). The Metropolitan Museum of Art, The Elisha Whittlesey Fund, 1957 (57.567). This engraving, which originally accompanied a treatise on new fire-fighting equipment, offers a wealth of information about Amsterdam interiors of the late 17th century. Note the kasten in upstairs rooms, one with a display of ceramics on the top.

two doors are flanked by side stiles and divided by a center stile attached to the right door. In some American examples the stiles are articulated by classical pilasters; in others their role as vertical supports is expressed by tall rectangular panels. The proportions of the cornice and the ball feet vary little from piece to piece. The base is usually constructed with exposed dovetails at the corners. Moldings in the shapes of rectangles, squares, and diamonds applied to the base echo the arrangement of doors and stiles on the main case.

This standard design bears some resemblance to that of well-known Baroque kasten from Amsterdam and other cities of the western part of the Netherlands, particularly the provinces of Holland and Zeeland. Both the American and the Dutch examples utilize a Baroque architectural framework related to doorway design and are raised off the floor by robustly scaled ball feet. At least seven monumental Dutch-made urban kasten have histories of ownership in the New York area going back to the seventeenth or early eighteenth century, making it tempting to attribute the origin of the American form to these opulent prototypes and others like them. The obvious differences between the American and Dutch kasten might be explained by the inequality between the levels of craftsmanship found in a small colonial outpost and in populous, flourishing urban centers in the homeland.

The American kast was thus a provincial interpretation of the grandiose veneered and carved urban Dutch kasten, produced by makers whose skills and tools were less sophisticated than those of craftsmen working in the cities of the Netherlands. However, it is not a certainty that the reinterpretation took place in America. A provincial level of craftsmanship existed in the Netherlands as well. In the northeast along the Dutch-German border, kasten quite similar in design and workmanship to the American ones have been found.[17] They have the same simplified Baroque design, without carved decorations or veneers and including an enlarged cornice, fielded panels on the doors, panels and glyphs on the stiles, and the reflection in the base of the divisions of the upper section.

In the seventeenth century this border area comprised the eastern parts of the Dutch provinces Overijssel, Drenthe, and Groningen and the western parts of the old German states in East Friesland, Westphalia, and the Lower Rhineland, although international boundaries shifted from time to time. Far removed from the expansive wealth of the mercantile centers along the coast, the area had a common culture, its inhabitants sharing the same traditional farming economy and speaking the same dialect. It is not at all impossible that emigrants from this part of Europe settled in the New York area, bringing with them their furniture-making traditions.[18] Further study is needed on this subject.

The Kast in America

Kasten in the New York and New Jersey area projected the same social and cultural values as did their counterparts in the Netherlands. These expensive pieces of furniture were the property of the wealthier members of the community and offered visual proof of their owners' substance. A kast was often part of a dowry, *uitzet* in Dutch. Simon Bogart of Staten Island stipulated in his will of 1746 that his wife receive "the cupboard that she brought into my estate."[19] In 1754 Abraham Adrianse of Dutchess County willed to his wife "all she brought to me, the cubbor and linnen."[20] In the same year, Nathaniel Townsend, a Long Island resident of English descent, left his wife "my cupboard, which I had of her."[21]

New Yorkers were as concerned as Netherlanders with the cleanliness of the home. In fact, the attitude of the Dutch in America, an isolated community under constant threat of being overwhelmed by the English, had much in common with the Netherlanders' view of their own situation. Admiral Maarten Tromp tied a broom to his flagship's bowsprit to symbolize his success in sweeping the seas of any enemies of the Netherlands, and the Dutch were proud to take the humble household brush as an emblem of their new republic, cleansed of past tyrannies.[22] A similar identification can be seen in America. Cleaning and scrubbing utensils are far more prevalent in New York inventories than in those from New England or the South. The 1686 inventory of Cornelis Steenwyck of New York City, for example, lists "4 brooms and 9 brushes, 13 scrubbing brushes, 31 rubbing brushes and 24 pounds of Spanish soap."[23] Over one hundred years later, Peter Gansevoort, the young scion of an old Albany family, wrote to his mother about the standards of his living quarters in Litchfield, Connecticut, where he attended law school: "I would rather dine in Baker's stable than in her [his landlady's] kitchen—yea much rather, for Baker's stable is cleaned daily, her kitchen not even annually. Now my squeamishness and good old Dutch habits, being as accustomed to as clean a Kitchen as a Parlour could not brook this."[24]

Travelers in New York State, like those in the Netherlands, noted the unusual preoccupation with immaculate order. In 1800 Albany was described as "antique, clean and quiet."[25] The doorknockers were scrubbed so thoroughly that they shone "like diamonds." Another visitor disapproved of the "old Dutch gothic" houses, but admitted that "they are kept very neat, being rubbed with a mop almost every day, and scoured every week."[26] This passion for maintaining a spotless house was so well known that Washington Irving included a satirical description of local housewifery in his *History of New York*. "The whole house was constantly in a state of inundation, under the discipline of mops and brooms and scrubbing brushes; and the good wives of those days were a kind of amphibious animal, delighting exceedingly to be dabbling in water."[27]

Listings in wills and inventories indicate that kasten in America served the same function as their counterparts in the Netherlands, being used primarily to store household linens. Among the objects that Albert Van Nostrand of New York City left his daughter in 1766 was "a cupboard and linnen."[28] Samuel Skidmore of Long Island left his wife "my cupboard and linnen."[29] Dutch household guides recommended the use of two strips of cloth on each shelf of the kast to cover the linen and prevent it from touching the wooden shelving or sides, a practice which must have been known in New York, as the inventory of Jacob De Lange lists "six cloths which they put upon the boards in the case."[30] One American kast still retains eighteenth-century labels assigning each space on each shelf to the proper linen: "best sheets," "old sheets," "guest napkins," and so forth.[31]

As in the Netherlands, Americans placed ceramic vessels on the tops of their kasten for decoration as well as for storage. The image of a kast supporting two large punch bowls and a vase of flowers is carved into the back of a spoon board from Bergen County, New Jersey (cat. no. 19). In 1711 Evert Van Hook of New York City left his wife "the new cupboard that is now amaking by Mr. Shaveltie, and the three great and twelve small earthen cups, that stand on the top of said cupboard."[32] Several decades later, Cornelius Van Duyn of Brooklyn willed his wife "the cupboard in the parlor, with the bowls thereon standing."[33]

The essential design of American kasten remained unchanged for over a hundred years. It was preserved as a recognized and valued embodiment of "Dutchness," much as the language with its old-fashioned dialect remained frozen in time. American Baroque kasten of the purest Dutch design were made in the most concentrated pockets of Dutch settlement, in several distinct local styles. The earliest examples seem to come from the area of Manhattan and western Long Island and from the upriver Dutch settlements at Albany and Kingston. From western Long Island the design traveled to Staten Island and central New Jersey as those places were settled. Kasten made along the western bank of the Hudson River, from northern New Jersey to Albany, are slightly more individualistic.

It is on the edges of the Dutch settlements, where the Dutch families associated and intermarried with English settlers, that the kast lost some of its Dutch character. A number of distinctive kasten descended in families from Queens and Nassau counties in central Long Island; of one-part construction, they have platform feet and austere facades with a minimum of moldings. In coastal Connecticut and along the New York-Connecticut border to Dutchess County, features of English architectural and furniture design were combined with the Dutch kast form, producing a series of interesting variations.

As early as the 1740s, Kalm had noticed that in New York City the younger generation spoke English, went to the English church, and described themselves as English, despite their Dutch names. This was less true in the farming communities, where land was not sold to outsiders and social life focused around the family and the local church, and where life remained largely unaltered for over a century.

The American Revolution caused the first significant break in this isolation. The Hudson River Valley witnessed occupation by both armies and clashes between them. Trade was disrupted; the agricultural markets in New York City virtually stopped functioning. It was difficult to remain neutral, and in the choice of sides there was no Dutch alternative. With independence and the growth of the new nation came immigration and westward expansion, removing even more barriers. Non-Dutch poured into New York City, Albany, and the countryside. The Dutch language became an ever greater anachronism, as the Synod of the Dutch Reformed Church recognized in 1790 when it formally discontinued services in Dutch. During the first quarter of the nineteenth century the remaining segments of purely Dutch society broke down.

The cultural and practical functions of kasten were disappearing, and gradually they ceased being made. Preserving textiles became less important to the nineteenth-century household when factories began producing inexpensive machine-made yardage of linen and cotton. Changes in architecture brought built-in cupboards and closets, and contemporary taste demanded English furniture forms. Social mores also changed regarding privacy. It was no longer proper to have a bed in the parlor, and one of the main purposes of the kasten, to store the bedding, was thus removed to a higher floor or a private bedroom.

Full-fledged Baroque-style kasten were produced in America into the first decades of the nineteenth century. The only signed kasten known were made after the Revolution by makers from areas outside New York City. They may well have been the last generation to build American kasten, the production of which had probably already ceased in the city itself.

No longer the vital symbol of a well-ordered household, the kast had come instead to stand for old-fashioned values and a Dutch heritage whose worth was seen as lessening and perhaps irrelevant in the young United States, with its forward-looking dynamism. Only a few old Dutch families sought to preserve the vestiges of their early colonial patrimony. It was after Dutch culture had been totally absorbed into American life, in the late nineteenth century, that a new antiquarian interest directed attention to the kast once again.

Joined Oak Kasten of the Seventeenth Century

It is axiomatic that highly valued rather than everyday furniture tends to survive for posterity. Therefore it should come as no surprise that the only known seventeenth-century-style case furniture attributable to New York is a group of five oak cupboards. Four of them, kasten in the Dutch tradition, are included in this exhibition (cat. nos. 1–4) and are the focus of this discussion. It is a small sampling indeed for a period of six or more decades in the life of a major early colony. The scarcity of artifacts and also of early records has left seventeenth-century-style New York furniture largely undefined. To begin to enlarge the area of our knowledge, the four kasten will be analyzed here and evaluated in relation both to contemporary work in the Netherlands and New England and to the type of American kast that developed subsequently.

The four kasten carry on the tradition of oak frame-and-panel joinery that dominated furniture construction in northern Europe and England from the fifteenth to the mid-seventeenth century and even later. Joined furniture, as it is called, was constructed of vertical stiles and horizontal rails enclosing panels set in grooves. Stiles and rails came together in mortise-and-tenon joints secured by wood pins. Thus, surfaces composed of a number of small panels characterized the New York kasten as they did the much more numerous New England cupboards and chests.

In the Netherlands, kasten made during the first half of the seventeenth century in the Mannerist and then the early Dutch classicist style were produced in joined oak. In the second half of the century, during the Baroque phase of Dutch classicism, oak was no longer the primary wood of choice, but oak and mortise-and-tenon joints remained in use for the structure of the cases, which were veneered. In America, the primacy of joined oak continued until about 1690, when, under the influence of Baroque-style furniture, paneled construction and the use of oak began to be displaced by different methods of construction and other native hardwoods. In kasten this change was reflected in the use of broad boards, mainly of red gum and yellow poplar, and the employment of dovetails to join the base. Thus in America the oak kasten are distinct from the eighteenth-century examples that followed them in type of wood and construction as well as in design.

Unlike American kasten of the eighteenth century, which although numerous are very similar in overall format, each of the four seventeenth-century examples presents a different interpretation of the common form. In this they reflect the diversity among kasten made in the Netherlands during the same century. However, because the American pieces display relatively simple joinery, while most Dutch kasten available for comparison are high-style products, a correlation between the two groups can in most instances be established only in general terms.

The type of kast favored in the Netherlands during the late sixteenth and the first half of the seventeenth centuries was a two-stage, four-door cupboard of vertical proportions (see fig. 3). One of the oak kasten, catalogue number 1, is a modest version and the sole American representative of this four-door type. It maintains the overall verticality of the Dutch pieces but not the marked discrepancy between the heights of the lower and upper cases nor the construction in two or more parts. The effect of its panels recalls Dutch examples of the mid-seventeenth century onward ornamented with applied moldings and beveled projections more than it does the earlier, richly carved two-stage kasten like the one shown in figure 3.[34]

By the mid-seventeenth century the other principal type of kast, with two large doors, was becoming dominant in the Netherlands. In its most elementary form, which goes back to Gothic cupboards, the doors are simply enframed top and bottom by a molding and at the sides by the front stiles.[35] Catalogue number 3 is structurally such a straightforward piece. The six vertical panels on each door and side correspond in proportions and number to those on paneled doors found in some seventeenth-century Dutch houses.[36]

Very often the two-door Dutch kast had a drawer spanning the bottom of the case (see cat. no. 7). Two of the oak kasten follow this format. The doors on each have two superimposed panels of equal size, but otherwise the kasten differ considerably. Catalogue number 2 is built in one piece and is small in comparison with the other three oak kasten, which are themselves of a lesser scale than most Dutch and eighteenth-century American examples. The kast is shown with the drawer (for which evidence remained) and most of the base conjecturally reconstructed. The second example with a drawer in the base, catalogue number 4, of the four oak pieces comes closest in design to urban Dutch kasten and most clearly reveals the form's architectural inspiration. Its top is closely related to the one in a design published by de Passe (fig. 4); it has the characteristic large ball-shaped front feet; and, like most Dutch examples from the mid-seventeenth century onward, it is constructed in three separate units: base, cupboard section, and top.

Joinery

Underlying these diverse expressions of the kast form are not only the unifying factors of their function and their stylistic source in the Netherlands, but also a common tradition of joinery. Certain characteristics of the joinery distinguish it from Anglo-American practices observable in New England furniture and reflect direct Continental influences. The most significant of these features are fielded panels, mitered mortise-and-tenon joints, moldings run on the framing members rather than applied, and the particular profile of the moldings.

Fielded Panels. The oak kasten all employ panels with four beveled sides that create a central field. The panels of three of the oak kasten (cat. nos. 1–3) are particularly distinctive not just because they are fielded but because there are two or more superimposed fields worked from the solid board, the inner field having a molded edge (usually a cyma reversa). Just such panels can be seen on the sides of some Dutch kasten, illustrated for example in figure 11.[37] With its ebony veneers, this kast (fig. 10) appears to be an urban product, as some room paneling from Amsterdam which also has double-fielded panels undoubtedly is (fig. 7). This type of panel occurs in rural work as well, for instance in case furniture from Germany near the Dutch border.[38] It would seem that panels like this were used in a broad spectrum of seventeenth-century work within the cultural sphere of the Netherlands and possibly beyond.

It is worth noting that the doors of a sizable group of American eighteenth-century kasten feature large double-fielded panels with cyma molded edges (see cat. no. 9). Double-fielded panels are not otherwise known in colonial American furniture and are not part of the Anglo-American joinery tradition. Fielded panels of any sort rarely appear in English seventeenth-century work before the 1660s or in New England before the end of the century, when single-field panels came into use.[39] An exception is provided by a few

10. Kast, Dutch, mid-17th century. White oak and ebony, H. 59 in. (149.9 cm). Museum of the City of New York. The kast has a history in the Wyckoff family of Brooklyn. The cornice has been reduced in height and the drawer and part of the base replaced.

earlier examples which have a single field with a molded edge; one of them may be the work of a Dutch joiner.[40]

Miter Joints. Like fielded panels, the miter joints seen on all the oak kasten are not characteristic of New England joined furniture but occur frequently in the Netherlands. In a miter joint the edges of two perpendicular pieces meet at a forty-five-degree angle. A mitered mortise-and-tenon joint is employed when the edges of the stiles and the rails enframing a panel are molded. It allows the moldings to meet at the joint on the miter (fig. 12, a). In Anglo-American work the moldings surrounding a panel are often made of separate pieces which are mitered and then applied. When moldings are worked into the solid wood, they occur on only one of the framing members or terminate before the joint; in either case, stile and rail come together in a flat-faced mortise-and-tenon joint (fig. 12, b).[41] This simpler joint is also found on the oak kasten, where it is used on side paneling.

Moldings. The molding on the framing members of all four oak kasten is a distinctive one consisting of a shallow ovolo with a bead, illustrated in figure 12, c. This profile is unknown in Anglo-American furniture.[42] It is, however, exactly the molding found on the front stiles and surrounding the double-fielded side panels of the Dutch kast shown in figures 10–11. It also figures on the edge of the top rear rail in the interior of the Dutch kast catalogue number 7 and on the members enframing the wall panel in figure 7. The profile seems to have been widely used in Dutch carpentry and joinery during the seventeenth century, on interior paneling and shutters and doors[43] as well as on joined furniture. The ovolo-and-bead profile has also been found on two grisaille-painted kasten (see p. 29) and run on the edges of boards on doors of the 1712 Jean Hasbrouck house in New Paltz, New York. As an applied molding, with the addition of an astragal on the outer edge, it surrounds panels on woodwork from that same house[44] and on the doors of a group of early- to mid-eighteenth-century kasten from Ulster County (fig. 39).

In the seventeenth century the ovolo-and-bead was characteristically worked on the edge of framing members or boards; it was not a profile used in applied moldings. A unique surviving example of seventeenth-century Dutch woodwork in New Netherland and an invaluable document is the pulpit of the First Church in Albany (fig. 13), sent by the Classis of Amsterdam in 1657. (Its panels have the arch motif found on many Dutch kasten as well as pulpits.) On the pulpit the ovolo-and-bead molding is worked on the edge of the members framing the horizontal and corner panels of the base. However, on the beveled moldings applied to those horizontal bottom panels, on the inner edge, there is a different profile—an astragal, a cove, and a bead—which is perpetuated in applied moldings on the front stiles and drawers of many eighteenth-century American kasten (see fig. 25).[45]

In the top moldings of the oak kasten the ovolo is the dominant profile, as clearly proclaimed by the salient convex frieze of catalogue number 4. This type of ovolo frieze is often found between the two stages of four-door Dutch kasten (see figs. 3, 5) and at the top of some low two-door examples from the first half of the seventeenth century.[46] Not only the frieze but the whole entablature—cornice, frieze, and architrave—crowning catalogue number 4 closely parallels the one in a design by de Passe (fig. 4). Such a three-part division also is evident, to a greater or a lesser degree, on the tops of the other kasten. On catalogue number 1 the uppermost panels serve as the frieze, and the molding

11. Detail of the side of figure 10, showing double-fielded panels and a broad sunken band on the upright

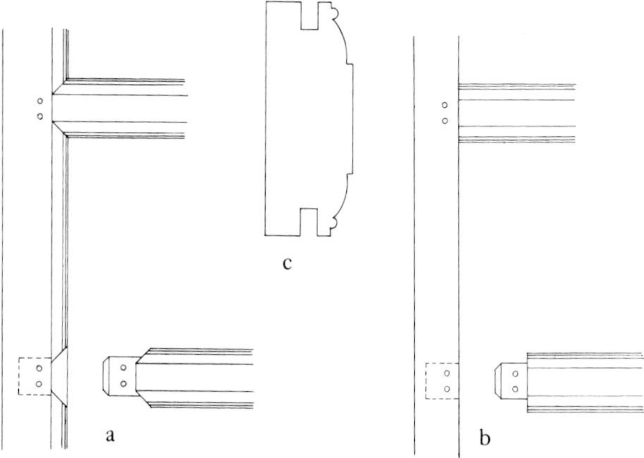

12. a: Miter mortise-and-tenon joint; b: Flat-faced mortise-and-tenon joint; c: Cross section of a rail showing ovolo-and-bead edge moldings and grooves to receive panels

below is similar to the architrave on catalogue number 4; however, the cornice, with its uppermost rectangular element, is atypical. Although on catalogue number 2 there is but a single massive top molding, the sequence of its profiles, beginning with an astragal dominating the cornice, followed by a large ovolo for the frieze, and ending with an architrave-like unit, still distantly reflects the divisions of an entablature. The single top molding of catalogue number 3 is similarly organized, except that it substitutes for the ovolo a large cyma reversa, which is the profile immediately above the architrave on both Dutch and American Baroque kasten.

A basic difference between the top moldings of the oak kasten and those of eighteenth-century American examples is that on the latter, cornice and frieze are not distinguishable; rather, a single expansive molding adjoins the architrave directly (Appendices B, C). There is continuity in the shapes of the architrave moldings, however, which, with certain modifications, carry on from the oak kasten to a number of eighteenth-century pieces (cat. no. 10).

On only two of the oak kasten do the bottom moldings survive (cat. nos. 3, 4): both have a prominent, fully rounded ovolo, above which rises a fascia with one or two fillets and then either a cavetto or a cyma (see Appendix D). A molding identical to that on catalogue number 3 appears on the 1657 Dutch pulpit in Albany below the base panels (fig. 13). Seventeenth-century Dutch base moldings may also feature a cyma (fig. 3) or a cavetto as the main profile. In New England joined furniture the cavetto predominates in base moldings, as it does on the English furniture from which it derived.[47]

On Dutch kasten of the second half of the century the ovolo becomes flattened and angles out sharply (cat. no. 7). In some of the American eighteenth-century examples, however, the ovolo characteristic of the oak pieces remains, with some small variations in scale and angle, the usual profile for the bottom molding. In the others a different profile such as the cyma is introduced (Appendix D). The preference of some New York woodworkers for the conservative ovolo is also evident in its presence on the bottom molding of the William-and-Mary style inlaid desk in the Museum of the City of New York, instead of the cyma above a broad fascia one would normally expect to see on a piece in this style.[48]

On those oak kasten where an upper base molding occurs (cat. nos. 1, 2, 4), the main components are an astragal and an ovolo, as they are for the corresponding moldings on some Dutch kasten (cat. no. 7) and above the base panels of the Albany pulpit (fig. 13). In eighteenth-century American kasten, however, the form is different, the upper base molding normally utilizing a cavetto rather than an ovolo (Appendix D).

Other Features. Several structural elements of the oak kasten—the backs, shelves, and hinges—should be noted, as they, too, seem to indicate a direct Dutch influence. Whether oak is the primary wood or is only used for the carcase, the backs of Dutch kasten are characteristically formed of vertical oak tongue-and-groove boards. Typically there is a board with two tongues near the center, tapered and often narrow, that most likely served as a wedge to force the backboards tighter together within the frame. The backs of catalogue numbers 1–3 all have a tapered piece. Since these backboards are totally or partially nailed, the value of a wedge for tightening the back may have been limited, but it still could have been an easy way to fill the space left by boards whose sides were not entirely parallel. There may also be a tapered section among the transverse boards of the top and bottom and the shelves of the American oak kasten.

The back of catalogue number 4 presents an interesting anomaly. It is made up of narrow riven oak clapboards simply overlapped and nailed (fig. 33). An analogy with house carpentry immediately comes to mind. Vertical boarding was common on the exteriors of Dutch wooden houses of the sixteenth and early seventeenth centuries and continued to be used on the gable ends of houses into the eighteenth century.

13. Pulpit, Dutch, ca. 1657. Oak. First Church in Albany, New York

Early views of New Amsterdam show vertical cladding on some houses.[49] The utilization of both tongue-and-groove boards and the less labor-intensive and therefore cheaper nailed clapboards is documented in a 1655 contract. The contract, which specified how a house on the Long Island side of the East River, to be occupied by the ferryman, was to be built, required that the front of the house "be planed and grooved" and that "the rear gable . . . have boards overlapped in order to be tight."[50]

As in Dutch prototypes, the shelves of the oak kasten are made of narrow boards running front to back, which are nailed to the top of a rear rail and to a recess on the upper back edge of a molded front rail (fig. 32). The rear rail is attached to the case by means of a joint, but the front one is not. On catalogue number 4, following Dutch precedent, the front rail is supported by brackets nailed to the front stiles. On catalogue numbers 2 and 3 the front rail was simply nailed directly to the stiles. In American eighteenth-century kasten rails were no longer needed, since shelf boards ran longitudinally and were set into the sides of the case.

The typical door hinge of a Dutch kast is a concealed iron pivot hinge (fig. 14). The same type appears on catalogue numbers 2 and 4 and is the standard hinge for eighteenth-century American kasten, but is not otherwise known in American furniture.[51] A butt hinge is used on the two other oak kasten; on catalogue number 3 it is attached in a distinctive way. Instead of being mounted in a recess on the surface, the hinge leaves are let into mortises in the door and case frames and then secured with nails. This type of attachment is atypical for American furniture and has been noted on only one other piece, a New York red gum desk (fig. 18). It does occur, however, on doors and shutters in the Netherlands.[52]

14. Detail looking down at a concealed pivot hinge of a kast (cat. no. 7). The iron strap secured to the bottom rail of the cupboard section extends to the left under the door, where it incorporates a cylindrical socket recessed into the rail. A pin projecting from a similar strap attached under the bottom edge of the door fits into the socket.

It seems clear, then, that the four oak kasten belong to a strain of oak joinery brought from the Netherlands and distinct from the joinery represented by New England furniture. The tradition appears to have been broad based—it is manifest in both furniture and interior house woodwork and extended beyond the present-day boundaries of the Netherlands, into Germany, for instance—but whether it was limited to the sphere of Dutch cultural influence or belonged to a wider tradition of northern European woodworking has not been determined. Certainly a proportion of the "Dutch" immigrants came from beyond the Netherlands proper, but from how far afield could immigrant woodworkers have brought a generically similar tradition? That other strains of Continental joinery existed in the colony in the seventeenth century is indicated by the one other joined case piece attributed to New York, an oak cupboard with a history of ownership in the Hewlett family of Merrick, Long Island.[53] The sources of its design have yet to be identified, but the piece relates directly neither to Dutch nor to English work.

Already in the first decades of the New Netherland colony, woodworkers of disparate backgrounds were present. The carpenter Juriaen Hendricks (Hendricksen) is identified in several house contracts, beginning in 1639, as being from Osnabrück (Germany); in 1641–42 at least three other men who contracted to build houses in the New Amsterdam area were identified as "English carpenters"; Jean Labatie, an exiled carpenter from France, was in Albany in the 1640s serving Rensselaerswyck and the West India Company.[54] The situation was fluid: craftsmen who worked for the company did not necessarily remain in the colony at the end of their contract, and other craftsmen did not always continue long in their trade.

The names of some seventeenth-century New York woodworkers, drawn from surviving records, have been compiled and on one occasion published, but much research remains to be done.[55] The most common designation for a woodworker during that period was "carpenter"; the term "joiner," for instance, indicating a maker of furniture, does not seem to have been used until the 1690s. The 1657 burgher list for New Amsterdam, for example, includes one chairmaker and eight carpenters.[56] Since someone must have been making furniture other than chairs, it is reasonable to assume that some of the men called carpenters were producing furniture. In the absence of guilds and with craftsmen at a premium, they were no doubt doing whatever work they were capable of performing.

Building and other types of contracts indicate that some carpenters were doing work requiring considerable skill. In 1661 the burgomasters requested Tomas Lambertsen (one of the carpenters on the 1657 list) and Sybrant Jansen to enlarge "the pew of Burgomasters and Schepens," using wainscot for which the city would pay.[57] Two years later Klas Tymmer was paid by the town of Flatbush not only for "laying the ceiling and hanging the bell" of the church but also for "making the reader's seat."[58] Some house contracts of the 1640s and 1650s include specifications for built-in bedsteads and cupboards, tongue-and-groove floors or ceilings, and the "wainscoting" of interior walls. The evidence of comparable wooden houses in the Netherlands suggests that this interior finishing was not panel-and-frame construction but rather vertical sheathing, with doors and shutters of vertical boards with battens or with an applied framework on one side to imitate paneling.[59] However, the skills and tools required to execute these commissions, such as crafting mortise-and-tenon joints, planing, and grooving, were ones that could also produce joined work. Thus the oak kasten could have been made by carpenter-joiners as early as the mid-seventeenth century.

The question of what level of demand the oak kasten filled can be addressed only in broad terms. On the one hand, the mere ownership of a large joined piece of furniture implies a certain standard of living. On the other, compared with Dutch high-style kasten the oak examples certainly fall into the category of provincial or simple urban furniture. Household inventories are scarce before the last two decades of the century. However, the more numerous later inventories strongly suggest that by the 1680s, joined oak furniture was no longer in fashion for the rich interiors of the merchant elite. When the wood of furniture from those households is mentioned, walnut is in strong evidence. Those kasten described as "Holland" or "of French nutwood" may be presumed to have been imported, as also furniture of ebony and "East India" pieces must have been.[60] The extent of importation in earlier decades, and among the average middle class, is not known. Some luxuries were locally obtainable well before the end of the century. During the 1670s New York City was already supporting several silversmiths. In 1675 there is mention of a woodworker with carving skills. More than a decade earlier the services of at least one portrait painter were available.[61] Whatever the demand oak kasten might have filled at an earlier date, it appears that if they were made toward the end of the century, they appealed then to the conservative middle class and not to the wealthier segment of the population.

There is little evidence to support anything but a broad range of dates, between 1650 and 1700, for the manufacture of these kasten. The main characteristics of their joinery—double-fielded panels and miter joints—were already in use in the Netherlands in the early seventeenth century. Features such as the paneled stiles of catalogue numbers 2 and 3 and the use of woods of contrasting colors as in catalogue number 4 are enunciated in de Passe designs of 1642 (fig. 5). Three-part construction appeared on Dutch kasten at mid-century, as did panels with bold applied beveled projections (see fig. 4 and cat. no. 7), which are recalled on catalogue number 1 by panels worked up in the solid and on catalogue number 4 by appliqués. Thus all the basic design elements of the oak kasten were present in the Netherlands by about 1650. On the other hand, the propensity of some of the New York population to retain old forms means that the oak kasten could have been made at the end of the century.

Stylistically, catalogue number 4 is without question the most advanced of the four kasten. The appliqués on its facade are of walnut, meant to contrast with the oak. Although walnut could well have been available in New York early on by way of contact with settlements in the Delaware Valley and trade with Virginia, the wood came into favor for furniture in the last decades of the century. The piece's three-part construction, ball front feet, and applied horizontal glyphs articulating the stiles are elements of design also present in American kasten of the eighteenth century.

Variety and Continuity in Eighteenth-Century Kast Design

The changes wrought in Dutch classicism as it passed from a late Renaissance into a Baroque phase are well illustrated by Dutch kasten made in cities of the northern provinces between the 1620s and the 1680s (figs. 3, 8). American kasten, provincial manifestations of the Dutch classicist style, underwent a similar design transformation at a lower level toward the close of the seventeenth century. Formerly constructed of small panels and frames of oak (cat. nos. 1–4), kasten began to be made of broad sawn boards of red gum, yellow poplar, and occasionally walnut or mahogany. New features were adopted, chiefly a large single-panel door format, an overscaled Baroque cornice, and the use of applied moldings rather than moldings run on framing members. Because they were produced over such a long period of time—the rare examples bearing a maker's mark date to the 1790s (fig. 19 and cat. no. 16)—American Baroque kasten survive in considerable numbers. So few are signed, labeled, or dated, however, that it is far easier to explicate differences and similarities among the many surviving examples than to speak with certainty about how or when this later version of the form first emerged.

Baroque-phase kasten are almost formulaic in overall appearance. Within the basic formula, however, there are variations in design which allow the almost two hundred examples to be divided into groups. The existence of groups of related kasten argues strongly for the theory that distinct local styles developed within a few larger schools of eighteenth-century kast-making in the Dutch cultural areas of New York and New Jersey. Intensive localized research has made it possible to identify an Ulster County style with a recognizable shop tradition centered in Kingston.[62] This local style seems to be part of a larger Hudson River Valley school that flourished on the west side of the Hudson in Albany, Greene, and Ulster counties, southern Rockland County, and Bergen County, New Jersey. A second major school apparently originated in Kings County on the western end of Long Island and spread from there to Staten Island and central New Jersey. A third distinct school that developed in the neighboring county to the east, Queens, was carried across Long Island Sound to southern coastal Connecticut and Westchester County, New York.

15. Detail, left door of kast (cat. no. 6)

New York City

There is much we do not know about where and by whom American kasten were made, for reasons that include the transportation of kasten away from their original places of manufacture (which took place even in the 1700s), devastating fires in Manhattan during the Revolution and the subsequent intense urbanization of the New York metropolitan area, and the dearth of documented examples already mentioned. Perhaps most critical is our ignorance of the role played by New York City as a center of kast production in the late seventeenth century. From at least the time of the English takeover of 1664 on into the early eighteenth century, the city's wealthy Dutch merchants and political elite—the people who undoubtedly exerted the greatest influence on the taste of the middle class—were importing elaborately carved and veneered Baroque kasten from the Netherlands for use in their homes. The 1691/92 estate inventory of François Rombouts, a former mayor of New York, lists five cupboards including "a holland Cubbert furnished with Earton ware and Parslin" valued at £15. Cornelis Steenwyck, reportedly the second wealthiest citizen of New Amsterdam at the time of the English takeover, had recorded in his estate inventory of 1686 that a "cupboard or case of French nutwood" valued at £20 occupied the "Great Chamber." Listed as contents of the same room were a square table valued at £10 and a looking glass at £6. The cupboard's value suggests that it was a high-quality, up-to-date piece, perhaps not very different from the kast in the Rijksmuseum dated 1689 (fig. 8) or the veneered and carved walnut example formerly owned by the Beekman family of New York City and now in the collection of the New-York Historical Society (fig. 35).[63]

It is not unlikely that by the 1690s middle-class burghers of modest means had begun asking local New York City joiners to produce kasten with some pretensions to the latest Dutch Baroque style. Only a handful of American kasten, however, show features that seem to be a response to the design of high-style Dutch Baroque kasten of the seventeenth century. Chief among these are the grisaille-painted ones with perimeter moldings discussed at length later in this essay, and also a few kasten of red gum, walnut, or mahogany, some with perimeter door moldings and all with paneled sides and applied pilasters (figs. 16, 17 and cat. nos. 6, 8).

Kasten with Perimeter Door Moldings. Perimeter door moldings are a standard feature of all seventeenth-century Dutch Baroque kasten. These moldings not only handsomely frame the doors but also offer some stability to the vertical-board substructure beneath the veneers, moldings, and carved ornaments that create such rich and dramatic effects. None of the American examples cited above is as elaborate or visually complex as its urban Dutch counterparts; nonetheless, it is instructive to compare one of them, catalogue number 6, with the Dutch kast imported for the Beekman family (fig. 35).[64]

The most striking similarity between the two is in their door designs; these differ only in the profile of the molding surrounding the central field, which is an ovolo on the Dutch example and a cavetto on the American one. The American kast even has the same broad mitered swaths of veneer between the central field and the perimeter moldings (fig. 15), a detail which makes it unique among surviving American kasten. Other design parallels are also evident, like the presence on both of flat paneled sides, applied rectangular panels behind the drawer pulls, a sharp chamfer at the base of the cornices with a large cyma reversa profile just above it, and (despite a considerable size differential) very similar overall proportions: the Dutch example is 87 inches tall and 88 inches wide, the American kast 77 inches tall and 79 1/2 inches wide. Such a thoroughgoing reinterpretation of a stylish Dutch Baroque kast of the late seventeenth century as catalogue number 6 offers probably could have been carried out only by a New York City joiner, who would have had both ample opportunity to see models like the Beekman family kast and a clientele eager to update an established form. But one cannot be sure that the design evolved in America. A similar process of adaptation was also under way in smaller towns and villages of the Netherlands, notably those in the eastern provinces, and the design could have been brought to New York fully developed as part of the design repertoire of an immigrant provincial Dutch joiner, perhaps as early as the 1680s.[65]

Only one other American kast with perimeter door moldings invites close comparison with late-seventeenth-century Dutch Baroque kasten like the one from the Beekman family or the Rijksmuseum example (fig. 8). This kast, from the Keteltas family of Staten Island and New York City (fig. 16),[66] is massive by American standards, measuring 85 1/4 inches in height and 84 inches in width at the cornice, with proportions similar to those of catalogue number 6

16. Kast, New York City, 1690–1720. Walnut, yellow poplar, and pine, H. 85 1/4 in. (216.5 cm). The Conference House, Staten Island, New York. The lower base molding and front feet of the kast appear to be replacements.

and the Beekman kast. Like catalogue number 6 it has molded surrounds with a cavetto profile on the central fielded sections of the door panels, but it lacks the broad swaths of mitered veneer. Two other noteworthy features that may indicate its manufacture at an early date in New York City are the kast's construction of solid walnut, the most fashionable wood of the 1680s and 1690s, and its removable cornice, doors, interior shelves, and paneled back, which allowed it to be disassembled. The desirability of a kast that could be knocked down may have followed from the practice of using kasten in second-floor rooms, which is documented for Amsterdam in an engraving of 1690 (fig. 9) and for New York City in the 1724 inventory of Gertruy Van Cortlandt, who at her death had "1 old Holland case" listed in "the chamber over the back parlor" of her tall, Dutch-style town house, a type of building found in the seventeenth century only in Manhattan and, in fewer numbers, in Albany.[67]

Catalogue number 8 also has perimeter door moldings, but its door panel design differs from those of previously discussed examples. Instead of small central fields isolated on a flat background, here there are panels articulated with multiple applied moldings and beveled sections of wood that project dramatically from the facade, in counterpoint to the boldly jutting cornice. Visually these panels seem more akin to the type found on Dutch Baroque *kussenkasten* like catalogue number 7 and communicate the vigor associated with the inception of a new style. Catalogue number 8 has a traditional history of ownership in Brooklyn and could have been made either there or in New York City in the early decades of the eighteenth century.

A fourth kast with design features that indicate an early date of manufacture possibly in New York City, but without perimeter moldings, is shown in figure 17. Like catalogue number 8 it has door panels built up with beveled sections of wood, but they are visually less complex and do not appear to project as dramatically from the facade because of their wide recessed centers. Like the three kasten with perimeter door moldings, this one has applied pilasters, paneled sides, and applied panels behind the drawer pulls. It also has a particularly strong ovolo-profile base mold-

17. Kast, probably New York City, 1690–1720. Mahogany, yellow poplar, and pine, H. 76 1/4 in. (193.7 cm). New York State Office of Parks, Recreation, and Historic Preservation, Guy Park State Historic Site

ing with an additional molded upper step reminiscent of that on an oak kast (cat. no. 4), another possible indicator of an early date. But the kast's most intriguing feature is its construction of solid mahogany. This makes it unique among American kasten and relates it to a small but important New York group of mahogany drop-leaf tables with robustly turned legs, some of which may date to the early 1700s.[68]

The Kings County School

While the kast shown in figure 17 is the only known American example made of solid mahogany, the wood is decoratively applied in plaques or panels to the front stiles of over fifty American kasten. In fact, the decorative use of mahogany, in combination with a distinctive double-fielded door panel design, is what separates and defines the largest school of American Baroque kasten. These kasten are tentatively attributed to Kings County, Long Island. Other distinguishing characteristics of the school include the consistent use of applied diamond-shaped plaques flanking and at the center of the base drawer; moldings—especially those in the architrave and above, below, and between the panels on the front cupboard stiles—consisting of a series of small-scale beads, fillets, cavettos, and quirks that give them a reeded appearance; slightly attenuated proportions, with most examples measuring five or six inches taller than their width at the cornice; and, generally, two-part construction, the first part a separate base unit with attached feet, the second a large cupboard section to which the cornice is affixed with glue and nails. The overall effect of kasten from this school is taut and planar due to the relatively low relief of the door panels; their applied moldings have a crisp, almost mechanical quality.

18. Detail of desk, probably Kings County, New York, 1695–1720. Red gum and yellow poplar, H. 35 1/2 in. (90.2 cm). The Metropolitan Museum of Art, Rogers Fund, 1944 (44.47)

The double-fielded door panel is a distinctively Dutch feature not found in any seventeenth- or eighteenth-century American case furniture outside the sphere of Dutch culture. It seems related to paneling, like examples from a seventeenth-century Amsterdam interior (fig. 7). Double-fielded panels appear in smaller scale on three of the joined oak kasten (cat. nos. 1, 2, 3), but the precise relationship between these and the double-fielded panels of expanded format has not been defined. It is quite likely that New York joiners who had previously utilized the double-fielded door panel design on a smaller scale in kasten of riven oak simply enlarged the design when they began working with larger sawn stuff and in an updated style.

The possibility that this particular school of kast-making originally developed in New York City cannot be discounted. However, at present the available evidence suggests that it was centered in Kings County on western Long Island, in the five originally Dutch towns—Brooklyn, Flatlands, Flatbush, New Utrecht, and Bushwick—which (along with Gravesend, an English settlement from the start) formed what is now the borough of Brooklyn. In the absence of any signed or labeled kasten by makers from the five towns, that evidence consists only of some examples with traditional histories of ownership by Brooklyn families and some related furniture forms also with Brooklyn histories, particularly an important desk on frame in the Metropolitan Museum (fig. 18).[69]

Written in chalk under the lid of the desk is the inscription "1695 Ocktober 12 gelient den P-Q maule Schenk 5 pont," a record of a loan of five pounds. According to museum records, the desk was purchased by a dealer in 1922 out of a house in the Cortelyou Road section of Flatbush in Brooklyn. If the history that accompanies the desk is correct and if the inscribed date is roughly contemporary with its manufacture, then the desk serves as a benchmark of sorts for this school of kast-making. Like number 9 in this catalogue and all the kasten with Brooklyn histories, the desk has mahogany-inset applied panels across its front. The molded battens under the lid are similar in character and profile to the architrave molding and applied horizontal moldings on the front stiles of catalogue number 9, and wood use in the two pieces is identical, with red gum the primary wood and yellow poplar used secondarily. But the most telling similarity is between the dovetail joinery in the upper carcase of the desk and that in the base of the kast. In both, the joints, precisely cut, have steeply pitched end-grain pins with thin necks. Even stronger evidence of the two pieces' origin out of a common shop tradition is the dovetailing in each instance of the front boards to the sides and the sides to the back. The result is the same pattern of face-grain tails and end-grain pins on the facades of the desk and the kast as on their exposed back corners. It is a pattern of dovetailing not common in American kasten outside this school and not typical of carcase construction in American case furniture altogether.

The contention that mahogany insets are a local characteristic of Kings County work is further supported by three clothespresses all with histories in the Dutch Long Island town of Flatlands.[70] The clothespress, a thoroughly English eighteenth-century furniture form, was very popular in New York City from about 1750 to 1800. Clothespresses from Flatlands are overlaid with ornament typical of kasten from the Kings County school, including overscaled cornices with crisply molded architraves, mahogany-inset applied panels on the front stiles flanking the cupboard section, and crisp, hard-edged applied moldings above and below the panels—all very similar in character to features found on kasten from this school. The fact that these clothespresses spring from English roots and date to the 1780s or later but still retain strong ties to a non-English design tradition established almost a century earlier suggests that both Brooklyn makers and their customers were reluctant to give up the strongly Dutch quality they were accustomed to having in case furniture, despite the march of time and its attendant social and political changes.

The Kings County school of kast-making was apparently brought to Staten Island and central New Jersey by settlers from western Long Island who migrated to those farming areas beginning in the late seventeenth century. Little is known of Staten Island kasten, but the few that survive in the collection of the Staten Island Historical Society have design attributes typical of the school. One from the Journeay family appears to come out of the same shop tradition as catalogue number 9, while a second with a history

19. Kast, made by Matthew Egerton, Jr., New Brunswick, New Jersey, ca. 1787–1802. Red gum, walnut, white and yellow pine, H. 76 1/2 in. (194.3 cm). Monmouth County Historical Association, Freehold, New Jersey

of ownership by the Seguine family of Rossville, a rather crude rendition of the type, reveals the hand of a carpenter unfamiliar with the fine points of Kings County school design and construction.[71]

In central New Jersey, Matthew Egerton, Jr. (ca. 1765–1837), made and labeled kasten essentially of the Kings County type (fig. 19), though his work gives evidence of the later period in which he worked and a certain misunderstanding of or distance from original design sources, employing bracket feet and brass drawer handles with oval backplates typical of late colonial and Federal era furniture. He also strayed from the base design of a single wide drawer with applied moldings, substituting for that two smaller drawers with lipped edges. Egerton's father, Matthew Egerton, Sr. (1739–1802), also a furniture-maker, in all likelihood had trained his son. Of English descent, Egerton senior married a Dutch woman; their children became members of the Dutch Reformed Church. Though no labeled kasten by the elder Egerton are known, he may have been the first in the family to make kasten for Dutch and Anglo-Dutch customers in and around New Brunswick. One other kast, now at the New Jersey State Museum in Trenton, which bears the signature of James Garretson and has a traditional history of ownership in Somerset County, New Jersey, appears to be based on the Kings County type, although it may be a local New Jersey product.[72]

20. Kast, Queens County, New York, 1720–50. Cherry, H. 72 ½ in. (184.2 cm). Roslyn Landmark Society, Roslyn, New York. This kast descended in the Kirby family of Roslyn, Long Island.

The Queens County School

A second Long Island school of kast-making, unrelated stylistically and structurally to the Kings County school, developed in adjacent Queens County. This part of the island was settled largely by people of English descent from New England; they maintained ties with their former communities but also interacted socially and economically with their Dutch neighbors nearby in western Long Island. By the early-eighteenth century Dutch families were moving eastward from Kings County into the Queens County towns of Hempstead and Oyster Bay. It is probably this direct intermingling of cultures which by the 1720s had given rise to a distinct Queens County school of kast-making.[73]

The Queens County style is marked by considerable ornamental diversity and some unusual structural features. Kasten range from extremely plain examples with totally unornamented facades (fig. 20) to others with applied panels on the front stiles and diamonds on the base (cat. no. 14), features typical of Dutch seventeenth-century design in the Netherlands. A freedom of expression prevails in this school of a sort not found among kasten in either the Kings County or the Hudson River Valley school, suggesting that makers in Queens County were not constrained by a given set of design principles inculcated by a few dominant shops or the expectations of a conservative clientele.

This is not to say that the designs were always successful. Against the standard of "Dutchness," Queens County kasten do not measure well. Their molding profiles and door panels appear to derive less from seventeenth-century Dutch classicist models than from early Georgian paneling and woodwork. The profile of the cornice on catalogue number 14, which is typical of many kasten of the Queens County school, has an upper cavetto with a break below and then a large ovolo profile essentially the same as that of bolection-molded fireplace surrounds of the early to mid-eighteenth century.[74] Noticeably missing from

21. Platform feet now supporting the kast shown in figure 20. They are not original to the piece, although they are old and inscribed with the date 1736.

cornices of the Queens County school is the distinctive sharp chamfer with a strong cyma reversa just above it which typifies kasten of the Kings County and Hudson River Valley schools and Dutch Baroque examples like catalogue number 7 (see Appendix C).

Though visually diverse, most kasten from the Queens County school share several distinctive structural features: one-part construction (fig. 41), separate platform feet, and a framed front. One-part construction is totally antithetical to the design of urban Dutch Baroque kasten, in which the base, central cupboard, and cornice unit are always separate. The separate platform feet may be Dutch in origin, however.[75] Instead of the four feet being attached separately, the front and rear feet on each side are connected to a board on which the entire cupboard rests (fig. 21). Platform feet are also used on another well-known furniture type from this area, the Long Island double-paneled chest. These chests were probably made by the same joiners who made the kasten, since in design and construction the two groups are similar. Both the chests and the kasten have substantial mortise-and-tenon front frames affixed with nails to board-constructed carcases. The approach even extends to a mid-eighteenth-century desk on frame from Queens County that has a fully paneled slant front and, even more surprisingly, a framed front on the lower carcase section, with drawer dividers that are tenoned into wide front stiles. The framed front makes for an ungainly piece of furniture, but clearly reveals the front-framing mind-set of makers working in Queens County.[76]

The non-Dutch aspects of Queens County kast design, as well as the preponderance of woodworking craftsmen with English names active there in the eighteenth century, suggest that English joiners played a major role in establishing the style of this school of kast-making. As the century progressed, both mixed Anglo-Dutch and purely English households commissioned kasten for their homes. Quite possibly made by English joiners and purchased by English families, kasten of the Queens County school are a tangible manifestation of the Anglo-Dutch cultural blending that was taking place in New York and New Jersey, in varying degrees, from the middle of the seventeenth century through the Revolution.[77]

It is documented that joiners were among those residents of Queens County who moved across Long Island Sound into Connecticut and Westchester County, New York, during the eighteenth century.[78] That fact probably explains the existence there of an interesting subgroup of the Queens County school. A group of eight kasten is known with unusual multi-paneled doors and false-paneled stiles flanking the doors, but no center stile; some, such as catalogue number 15, also have a double range of drawers below the doors. A number of these kasten were found in the Connecticut towns of Stamford, Greenwich, New Haven, and Litchfield, which, like central Long Island, had a mixed Anglo-Dutch population.[79] Noteworthy is the free use of English-type brass drawer pulls and keyhole escutcheons, from which some of these kasten can perhaps be dated to the 1760s or 1770s but not much earlier. The form has much in common with English and Welsh clothespresses and with some clothespresses from Pennsylvania, such as an example at Yale which is said to represent "a significant merger of Continental and Anglo-American traditions."[80] It is possible that kasten like catalogue number 15 were derived in the final quarter of the eighteenth century from Queens County school kasten with platform feet, already in use in southern coastal Connecticut or Westchester County, by an immigrant joiner recently arrived from Wales or

22. Detail of left front foot and base section of kast (cat. no. 11), showing glyph above base

England—thus adding still another layer of British interpretation to an already hybrid Anglo-Dutch form.

Kasten having features associated with the Queens County school are also known in Dutchess and Orange counties in New York, other areas that attracted settlers from Long Island throughout the eighteenth century.

The Upriver Hudson Valley School

On the west side of the Hudson River to the north, in Ulster, Greene, and Albany counties, the land continued to be owned by descendants of the region's original Dutch settlers until after the Revolution. Here, especially in Ulster County, a school of kast-making thrived that is almost purely Dutch in character.

Not very much is known about kasten made in Albany, since few kasten with Albany histories survive. A kast of red gum that descended in the Van Rensselaer family and is now at the Albany Institute of History & Art may have been made in Albany. It has door panels built up of separate beveled sections of wood and multiple applied moldings on a flat subpanel.[81] In fact, the main identifying characteristic of the upriver Hudson Valley school is the design of its door panels, essentially a simplified interpretation of the heavily built-up type found on Dutch Baroque kasten like catalogue number 7.

Ulster County. The area that has yielded the most information about this particular school of kast-making and its eighteenth-century pattern of development is Ulster County, which has only recently begun to witness the suburban sprawl that has transformed the landscape of the New York metropolitan area. Here it is possible to identify a body of surviving kasten still owned by local families and local institutions, on the basis of which a viable design chronology may be developed and the attributes of a distinct local style discerned.

In addition to built-up door panels, several ornamental features aid in the identification of Ulster County kasten. One is the design of the turned front feet, usually a large, slightly flattened ball shape with a moundlike swelling on the top (fig. 22). A second identifying feature is the cornice, which always has an astragal and a large cyma recta at the top, a strong central fascia, and a large cyma reversa and a sharp chamfer below (Appendix C). The architrave molding is a plain fascia surmounted by either an astragal (see cat. nos. 10, 12), similar to that on the oak kast catalogue number 4, or a cavetto, like that on catalogue number 11. The front stiles of the cupboard section most often carry applied panels, although sometimes they have pilasters (cat. no. 10). The short horizontal moldings at the top, center, and bottom of the stiles are one of two distinct types: either a glyph of the kind found in Mannerist ornament (fig. 22),[82] nearly identical in profile to the large vertical one on the left door of the design for a kast engraved in 1642 by Crispin de Passe the Younger (fig. 4); or one seemingly shaped by a sash plane, with a central fillet balanced by ovolos on either side (cat. nos. 12, 13).

Finally, it is noteworthy that Ulster County kasten lack an ornamental feature consistently found on kasten from both the Kings County and Queens County schools: English-style brass hardware. Throughout the eighteenth century, Ulster County makers eschewed the use of exposed brass drawer pulls and keyhole escutcheons, opting instead for turned wooden pulls, a sliding glyph on the center stile that covers the keyhole for the door lock, and concealed door hinges of a type found on all Dutch Baroque kasten (fig. 14). The sliding keyhole cover is the functional equivalent of the entire center half-column that slides to the right to reveal a keyhole on earlier Dutch Baroque kasten like catalogue number 7, or the piece of carved ornament that pivots to expose the keyhole on the center stile of some later Dutch Baroque examples (fig. 35). The continued use in Ulster County of a sliding glyph, wooden pulls, and concealed pivot hinges seems to be the expression of a strong preference for Dutch traditions and a conscious rejection of non-Dutch stylistic innovations.

Ulster County society remained ethnically homoge-

23. Side of the base drawer of kast (cat. no. 10). The two nails at the lower edge are modern additions.

neous and tradition-bound throughout the eighteenth century.[83] The original farming settlers came to the region in the 1650s from the colony of Rensselaerswyck to the north, where they had been unable to purchase property.[84] Kingston (formerly Wiltwyck) was the hub of settlement and remained the only important center of trade and government in the county throughout the 1700s. After a series of bloody skirmishes in the 1660s between the immigrants and the native population, known as the Esopus Wars, settlement finally took root west and south of Kingston in the rich bottomlands that lined the valleys of the Esopus Creek and Wallkill River, and a timeless agricultural life began for the Dutch inhabitants. According to Helen Wilkinson Reynolds, Ulster County was a place where "families remained for generations upon one farm or in one locality and transmitted from generation to generation the established ways of the community."[85] Just such an established tradition was the most impressive surviving object of their material culture, the Ulster County kast, which displayed only subtle changes in design over the entire course of the eighteenth century.

The consistency of structure and overall design and the enduring Dutch character of Ulster County kasten can only be explained by the continuing existence of a dominant shop steeped in Dutch design and joinery traditions, probably located in Kingston. Although no signed or labeled kasten by Ulster County makers have so far come to light, it is known that two Dutch families of woodworkers practiced in Kingston throughout the eighteenth century; most likely they were responsible for developing and maintaining the distinct Ulster County style.

The first is the Elting family, whose progenitor, Jan Elting (1632–1729), came to New Netherland in 1657 from the province of Drenthe in the northeastern part of the Netherlands. He seems to have begun on Long Island; in 1662 a debt to him for wainscoting a seat, possibly a church pew in the Reformed Church in Flatbush, is recorded in the Flatbush town records. By 1672 he was in Kingston, where he married Jacomytje Slecht. Together they had three sons, at least one of whom, William (bapt. 1685–1744), apparently carried on the family woodworking tradition in Kingston. William in turn provided his son Hendricus (bapt. 1722–?) with the wherewithal to pursue a woodworking career by a bequest in his will of a handsaw, a broadax, an auger, a scraping iron, and two planes described as the best in his shop.[86] The men-

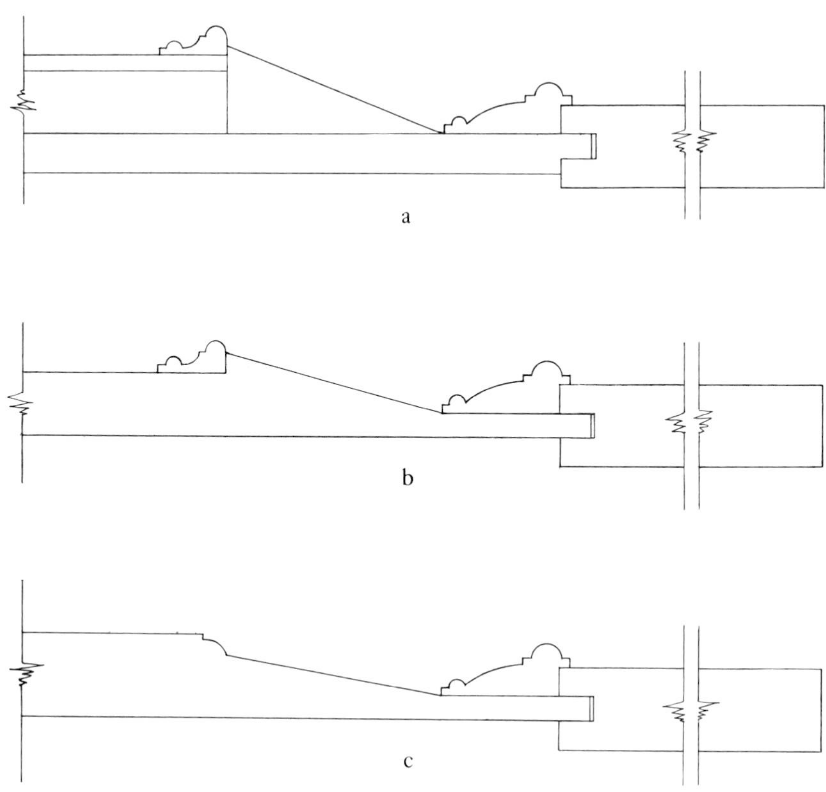

24. Cross sections of the three types of door panel found on Ulster County kasten

tion of the scraping iron is particularly significant because it implies that a part of the Eltings' work was bringing hardwood to a finished smoothness, a procedure requisite to the making of quality furniture. Two of Hendricus's older brothers, William, Jr. (bapt. 1713–after 1770), and Jacob (bapt. 1717–after 1770), were also woodworkers in Kingston, although by 1770 they had apparently specialized, since they are described then as "turners" in a jury selection list.[87]

The Beekmans were the second important family of Dutch furniture-makers active in Kingston during the eighteenth century. Their progenitor was Wilhelmus Beekman, who came to New Netherland from the province of Overijssel in 1647 and was a minor Dutch government official, first at the early Dutch settlement in Delaware and then in Wiltwyck (Kingston). He apparently maintained a residence in New York City, where six of his nine children were baptized. His third son, Johannes (1656–1751), of whom little is known, moved from New York to Kingston in 1699; Johannes's son Thomas (1689–1759) is the first Beekman known to have made furniture in Kingston. A will dated 1714 specifically cites him as the maker of "*Een neuive Cleere Kas*" (a new clothing cupboard) and "*Een neuive Tafell*" (a new table), and the minutes of a meeting of the Ulster County Board of Supervisors held in 1728 record a payment to him for a "chest to keep the County Records in."[88] Thomas Beekman probably trained his son, Cornelius (1733–after 1770), who by 1770 may have been the premier furniture-maker in Kingston, since he is the only one of the eleven woodworkers on the jury selection list (which names seventy-three Ulster County citizens in all) whose occupation is given as "joiner." One of Cornelius Beekman's four sons, Thomas (1761–1814), who is remembered in a nineteenth-century Ulster County history as a "carpenter by trade who also made coffins" and who represents a third generation of Beekmans active in Kingston, was possibly the last of the clan to make kasten.[89]

25. Detail of right foot and base section of kast (cat. no. 16)

Whether the matrix for the design of the Ulster County kast was Jan Elting's shop or Thomas Beekman's remains uncertain. Some features of these kasten seem quite early, like the Mannerist-style applied glyphs and the purely Dutch ovolo-and-bead profile found in the applied bolection moldings on the door frames (figs. 22, 40). These details may argue for the Elting shop, since it appears to have been established first and had as its master a first-generation Dutch joiner. Thomas Beekman, on the other hand, probably trained in a shop that was also rooted in the seventeenth-century Dutch design tradition. Tentatively, therefore, the bulk of the surviving Ulster County kasten are attributed jointly to the Elting and Beekman shops.

Kasten by the Elting-Beekman group of makers (cat. nos. 10, 11, 12) display consistent structural features. All are built in three parts with a separate cornice, cupboard section, and base unit. Red gum is the most common primary wood, but maple and sycamore are used in some later examples. Pine and yellow poplar are the secondary woods. The pattern of the dovetail joinery in the drawers and the placement of the channels that engage the drawer guides in the base unit are always the same; an example is illustrated in figure 23.

Two unusual features are the drawer front's sharply beveled top edge and ends, and the thin wooden wedges or slips which are driven between the dovetail keys to tighten the joints. Wooden slips or splines are also typically inserted in the front edges of the cornice miter joints. Tenons in the door-frame joints always pass completely through the stiles and are wedged top and bottom at the exposed ends but are never pegged. Wooden pegs are used, however, to secure backboards to the back edges of the cupboard shelves and to attach the front stiles and rails that frame the door opening to the sides and bottom board of the cupboard section. Wedged tenons and wooden pegs used as fasteners have been cited as hallmarks of German joinery when they occur in Pennsylvania furniture.[90] Jan Elting's native province of Drenthe was on the German border; it is possible that these techniques were well known there and that he brought them to Flatbush and Kingston.

In the course of three generations the Elting-Beekman makers produced kasten of a remarkably stable and enduring type. Changes over time can be detected, however, in the increasingly expedient methods used to make door panels and in a general lessening of ornamental vigor—essentially a design devolution.

Panels on the earliest Ulster kasten (cat. nos. 10, 11) are made in one of two ways: either they are built up from separate beveled sections of wood and multiple moldings applied to a flat subpanel as in figure 24, a, or a recess is plowed in the center of a solid fielded panel, as in figure 24, b, and then the moldings are applied. The latter method gives the essential look of the built-up type but reduced labor considerably. On later kasten (for example, cat. no. 12), even simpler door panels are found. These, too, are formed from a solid board, but instead of having a recess the central field is left proud, and a molding is worked around the perimeter, as in figure 24, c.

Bergen County. Approximately a dozen related kasten having fielded door panels with recessed centers can be attributed to Bergen County, New Jersey, on the basis of an important example signed by Roelof Demarest (cat. no. 16) in the late eighteenth century. All of these kasten appear to be of similar vintage, the evidence being the use of brass drawer handles with rosette or oval backplates and in some cases even more overtly Neoclassical ornament, such as inlaid paterae and other carved and molded designs typical of Federal architecture and decoration in Bergen County. Some structural and minor ornamental variations among the kasten suggest that they came from more than one shop, but overall their design is consistent and recognizable.

Kasten in the local Bergen County style all have door panels with recessed centers formed by beveling

26. Kast, Bergen County, New Jersey, 1790–1810. Cherry, H. 75 ¾ in. (192.4 cm). From the collections of Henry Ford Museum & Greenfield Village

a solid board on four sides to create a center field and then applying a heavy mitered molding around the field, as on catalogue number 16. The distinctive front feet are usually slightly ovoid balls (fig. 25). The diamonds applied to the base unit are smallish and slightly elongated. The upper molding on the base is made up of two pieces (the top one is attached to the cupboard section), while the profile of the lower molding is dominated by a wide, angled fascia surmounted by a slightly more than quarter round ovolo and a cavetto. Cornices are generally similar in appearance to the Ulster County type but lack the strong central fascia and well-defined upper astragal (for profiles of base moldings and cornices, see Appendices C, D). The front stiles are always articulated with panels, and in most examples the applied horizontal moldings on the stiles are characterized by a central astragal that protrudes noticeably at the ends.

Isolating these features in the signed Demarest kast and in other kasten with local histories in Bergen County[91] allows a number of interesting examples, which in the past were only generally described as New York work, to be attributed as well to Bergen County. A handful of kasten with compass inlays (fig. 43)[92] have door panels, cornices, and other base unit ornamental details typical of Bergen County local style. One particularly exuberant example (fig. 26) with compass inlays on the door panels, despite its uncharacteristic feet and lower base moldings, can also be attributed to Bergen County on the basis of its cor-

27. Corner cupboard, Bergen County, New Jersey, 1810–25. Pine, H. 90 in. (228.6 cm). Collection of The Newark Museum, Purchase 1964, The Members' Fund

nice design, two-piece waist molding, and door panels. These are made in the typical Bergen County fashion but clearly betray in the inverted corners, also repeated on the base drawer, a new interest in Neoclassical detailing. Inverted corners are found in Federal-style architectural woodwork from Bergen County, for instance, the door panels in the lower half of a corner cupboard dating to about 1815 (fig. 27), which also has gouge-work dentils flanking its arcaded baseboard that are very similar to those on the carved architrave molding on the kast in figure 26.[93] The relatively late date of this kast and the documented Demarest example, which probably could not have been made much before 1790, suggest that in the late eighteenth century Demarest and a few other Bergen County makers seized the kast form as their own and, taking a Neoclassical perspective, attempted to breathe some new life into it before its final demise.

Grisaille-Painted Kasten

Painted decoration representing large pendants of fruit in niches, executed mainly in blue-gray, white, and black in a technique known as grisaille, distinguish a small number of kasten. No doubt because of this striking decoration, these pieces have attracted more attention than any other American examples. The sculptural effect of their painted ornament and the Baroque opulence of its festoons and pendants are without parallel in other American kasten or in any other colonial painted furniture. Although these kasten clearly belong together by virtue of their decoration and their construction mainly of yellow poplar and pine (suggesting that they were meant to be painted), they present considerable variation, both structurally and in the details of their decoration.

The grisaille kasten fall into several structural

28. Grisaille-painted kast, probably New York City, 1700–1730. Yellow poplar, painted, H. 69 7/8 in. (177.5 cm). Courtesy, Henry Francis du Pont Winterthur Museum

groups. One group is distinguished by a bold ovolo containing a drawer in the frieze area of the top. A frieze of this type has its source in Dutch oak kasten of the late sixteenth century and the first half of the seventeenth, although it still occurs in Dutch painted furniture of the eighteenth century. Three kasten with a convex frieze, one of them catalogue number 5, can be linked to oak kasten by other features as well. For example, the nearly square overall proportions and the prominent ovolo profile of the base molding of this kast relate it to catalogue numbers 3 and 4. While these grisaille pieces are entirely of nailed board construction, their feet being simple extensions of the side and front boards, two of them (cat. no. 5 and another in the Metropolitan Museum, 23.171) do include some oak, notably in the backs of the cases, which show the same unusual use of nailed clapboards as the back of catalogue number 4 (fig. 33). The same two also carry the ovolo-and-bead molding characteristic of all the joined oak kasten. Structural losses and restorations on two kasten (MMA 23.171 and one in Gracie Mansion) preclude serious speculation about whether the three were made in the same shop.[94] A fourth kast with an ovolo drawer in the frieze area (private collection, Troy, New York) stands apart from the other three, having no particular ties to the oak examples in construction or molding profile and being vertical in its overall proportions.[95]

Figure 28 shows one of three grisaille kasten that constitute another group. Their design, with its bold overscaled cornice, drawer in the base, turned front feet, and applied horizontal moldings on the stiles, closely follows the well-defined formula of American Baroque examples (except for being about five inches shorter). Like a large group of their counterparts without decorative painting, these kasten are slightly taller than they are wide and are built in two sections: the cupboard unit, which is nailed or pegged together, with the cornice attached; and a dovetailed base, to which the feet are affixed (see, for example, cat. no. 9). Because these three pieces vary significantly in the dovetailing of the base, construction of the drawer, and profile of the cornice and manner of its attachment, one must conclude that they came from different shops.[96] They have, however, two distinctive features in common: a bottom molding with a cavetto profile, otherwise unknown in American kasten, and the particular construction of the doors, which is very unusual in American examples.

Each door consists of a single large board with a substantial perimeter molding on the exterior that frames the door visually and serves to stabilize the board structurally. As noted previously, this method of construction is common among Dutch kasten of the second half of the seventeenth century but exceptional for American ones, whose doors are virtually always framed. In the Netherlands the profile of perimeter door moldings varied: the oak kast with ebony veneers (fig. 10) has an ovolo, the *kussenkast* (cat. no. 7) a cyma. The profile characteristic of kasten like figure 8 is the cavetto, which is also found on the few unpainted American Baroque kasten that have perimeter door moldings. The same profile appears on the grisaille kasten. Interestingly, on catalogue number 5 and the related kasten at Gracie Mansion and in Troy, a perimeter molding is represented in paint.

Thus this latter group of Baroque-style grisaille pieces not only agrees in overall format and manner of construction with contemporary examples without painted ornament, but also incorporates in the treatment of the doors a feature of high-style Dutch work rarely found in American kasten. This perimeter molding does not occur, either in actuality or in painted facsimile, on Dutch grisaille kasten; nor is the deep cavetto characteristic of Dutch polychrome cupboards with moldings on their doors.[97] It thus appears that veneered Dutch Baroque kasten were the source of the feature. The probability is that these American grisaille kasten were made in shops where unpainted hardwood examples were also produced by craftsmen who were familiar with urban Dutch kasten—either through their own training or from imported works. The most likely setting for such shops is New York City.

A last structural category includes two pieces, one at Van Cortlandt Manor in Croton-on-Hudson, New York, and one in the Metropolitan Museum (42.73).[98]

29. Grisaille-painted kast, Dutch, probably late 17th or early 18th century. The kast is known only through this illustration from a 1914 article on old Zaan folk art (see note 103).

They are simple board cupboards offering no evidence of Dutch influence in either design or construction and come under consideration as kasten entirely by virtue of their painted decoration.

The decorative motifs that adorn the grisaille kasten—niches, pendants and festoons of fruit, drapery swags, foliate scrolls, rosettes, and an occasional cherub—are all part of a Renaissance vocabulary of architectural ornament that spread from Italy throughout northern Europe during the sixteenth and seventeenth centuries, primarily in the form of published designs. The ornamentation was found not only on architecture but also on furniture, metal objects, and work in other mediums. By the end of the seventeenth century these motifs appeared in Boston and New York, although their use was not widespread.[99] In no other instance does this ornament dominate the design as it does on these painted kasten.

In the Netherlands in the seventeenth century, this type of decoration was particularly associated with the architecture of Jacob van Campen (see fig. 6) and his followers, especially the interior work with its carved festoons and pendants (fig. 7). The carved ornament on

30. Grisaille-painted kast, Dutch, 18th century. H. 67 3/8 in. (171 cm). This kast, formerly in the collection of the Openluchtmuseum, Arnhem, was destroyed during World War II.

Dutch Baroque kasten like figure 8 is directly related to this school of architecture. So, too, is some of the carved ornament on a walnut cupboard or cabinet on stand, which provides an even closer link to grisaille kast decoration.[100] The cupboard has two niches draped with carved swags and pendants on its front and one on either side; in front, in the center, is carved a large pendant attached by a ribbon to a ring. The pendant is composed of miscellaneous objects, among which a wicker cradle is clearly recognizable. In the lying-in room of a late-seventeenth-century Dutch dollhouse stands a similar cupboard, also on a stand, with statuettes of Faith and Hope in niches on the front but without other carved ornament.[101] The grisaille painting on the Dutch kast shown in figure 29, with its figures of Minerva and Juno in niches on the doors, must seek to replicate cupboards of this sort. Its theme is similar: Juno is the protectress of women and goddess of marriage and childbirth. Every other known grisaille kast, whether Dutch or American, has in its niches not figures but pendants of fruit, a motif that makes fewer demands on the painter. In the center of many of the pendants is a large pomegranate, an attribute of Juno and a symbol of fertility. It is very likely that these kasten were dowry pieces.

The representation of sculpture or relief ornament by means of grisaille was a technique widely used in the Netherlands in the seventeenth century for decorating the interiors of both private houses and public buildings. Thus by mid-century the motifs of the van Campen school were also to be seen in paint, supplementing or replacing carved woodwork. Grisailles were also painted on canvas and mounted on plaster walls to simulate carved stone. The paintings depicted not only ornamental motifs, such as festoons of flowers and leaves, but also niches containing sculptures representing Roman deities and allegorical figures.[102]

While grisaille painting and its ornamental vocabulary were well established in the Netherlands, Dutch kasten decorated in grisaille are now a distinct rarity. The kasten in figures 29 and 30 are known only through photographs.[103] There is one four-door kast in a museum in Enkhuizen, and another with two doors has turned up in New York.[104] However, it is known that already in the second half of the seventeenth century there was extensive production of painted furniture in the Netherlands, supplying both urban and rural markets with an economical alternative to hardwood pieces. In Amsterdam, for instance, a separate group of craftsmen (*witwerkers*) was permitted to work only in softwoods, making inexpensive furniture which was then decorated by painters.[105] But because little Dutch painted furniture has survived (what has is primarily polychrome dated to the eighteenth century or later), the exact character of seventeenth-century painted furniture remains elusive. To what extent high-style furniture was closely translated into paint, as in figure 29, and with what speed changes in fashion were reflected in this medium, remain unanswered questions.

That the grisaille painting on American kasten was executed by specialists is implied by the similarity of the decoration on several dissimilar kasten. Five kasten—two with a drawer in the top (cat. no. 5 and the one in Gracie Mansion) and the three with a drawer in the base (fig. 28 and ones at the Monmouth County Historical Association and Van Cortlandt House in the Bronx)—show closely related compositions and painting styles and must have been decorated in the same shop or associated shops. In each case the large pendant of fruit is organized around a central pomegranate or pear that rests on a large leaf, above which are four symmetrically placed apples (if that is what they are meant to be); to the sides hang bunches of grapes, and below are apples mixed with grapes; tendrils curving up from either side provide perches for a pair of birds. Festoons and smaller pendants elsewhere on the kasten are almost always made up of four apples arranged to form a lozenge. The painting is in black and white on a blue-gray overall ground. The fruit is painted in a consistent manner, with the volume of an apple similarly defined and highlighted in all five kasten, and the spot of its flower end virtually always facing four or five o'clock.

Some variation in other details of the decoration, however, could be interpreted as a weakening of the tradition. For example, the motif of acanthus leaves flanking the festoons—found on the convex frieze of every Dutch kast (figs. 29, 30)—is rendered recognizably in the center of the frieze drawer of catalogue number 5 but has lost its architectural connotation at the drawer ends; wrapped around the corner, it no longer has the appearance of a capital surmounting a column or pilaster. On the three American kasten with a drawer in the base, this motif is poorly delineated or replaced by nondescript foliage (fig. 28), while the pendants in the niches seem to be suspended in space rather than being more plausibly attached to a ring or the keystone of the arch, as in catalogue number 5.

The present rarity of Dutch grisaille kasten permits only a very limited comparison to be made between this body of American grisaille decoration and its Dutch counterparts. The vocabulary of ornament of the two groups is quite similar, as is the arbitrary use of light and shade in the niches. The swags with four apples on the Dutch kast with statuettes (fig. 29) are very close to those on the American pieces, and the Dutch kast now in the United States provides a precedent for the placement of a pear at the center of a pendant, as on catalogue number 5. However, on the whole, painting on the Dutch kasten is more elaborate and, except for the one with statuettes, generally darker; the kast in Enkhuizen is executed entirely in black and white, without any gray. Certainly the rendering of the fruit, for instance, on figure 30 and the Enkhuizen kast is not at all similar to that on the American examples. Nevertheless, the overall dependence of the American work on Dutch prototypes is indisputable.

The relative competence of the painting on these five American kasten and their manufacture by several different woodworkers, some of them aware of Dutch Baroque examples, seem to place this American school in the largest center of the province, namely New York City. Unfortunately, family histories to corroborate this hypothesis are lacking.

The other American grisaille kasten were decorated with varying levels of skill by painters following, more or less closely, the conventions used by the presumed New York school. A kast in the Metropolitan Museum (23.171) that is structurally in the same group as catalogue number 5 shows much emphasis on the details of ribbons and foliage and a niche that extends to the bottom of the door, which lacks a painted perimeter molding. The niche is shaded in the usual manner to suggest depth, but the pendant is a somewhat awkwardly arranged affair with little three-dimensionality. The kast with a drawer in the top in Troy is distinguished by additional motifs: winged cherubs' heads above the arches, vases of flowers at the bottoms of the stiles, and various animals and insects around the pendants on the doors. The doors have a painted perimeter molding recalling catalogue number 5, but the rather inexpert painting and overloaded swags of fruit place this decoration at some remove from that of the dominant American shop. The simple board cupboard in Van Cortlandt Manor presents a somewhat different combination of motifs by yet another painter, including angels, a spray of leaves defining each arch, bowls and vases of flowers, and a tulip extending from the top of each stile pendant. The painting style, the procumbent angels above the arches, the birds' stance, and the introduction of red and yellow tones all connect this work to a cradle seemingly decorated by the same painter. On both the cupboard and the cradle (whose decoration also includes a group of figures, probably a biblical scene),[106] the well-worn paint may have been applied with greater technical skill than is now apparent.

Finally, there is the Metropolitan Museum's plain board cupboard (42.73), which is decorated in quite a different manner. Large acanthus scrolls incorporating flowers, grapes, and birds run vertically on the doors and sides like a giant border. A similar use of the motif occurs between paired caryatids in the courtroom of the Amsterdam Town Hall.[107] It also appears on the sides of some polychrome decorated kasten in the Netherlands, placing this piece within the Dutch tradition. This kast is painted in monochrome shades of brown, not gray like the other American kasten. In the Netherlands much seventeenth-century architectural grisaille was done in brown, and while gray seems to have predominated in the eighteenth century, both colors continued in use.[108]

The dating of the grisaille kasten must remain tentative. No documentation is available on any examples, either Dutch or American, and both the decorative vocabulary and the painting technique they display remained current in the Netherlands for an extended period of time. Many of the same motifs appear there on polychrome furniture, some of which has been dated to the mid- to late eighteenth century.[109] Grisailles continued to be popular in interior architecture during that century as well.[110] One starting point for arriving at a date is the premise that carved walnut cupboards with niches were the inspiration for grisaille pieces like figure 29, and that such walnut cupboards date probably to the last three decades of the seventeenth century (see n. 100). One might then suppose that this type of grisaille painting of kasten was established in the Netherlands by the end of that century. How soon such furniture was being either imported to New York or made there by craftsmen with Dutch training is a matter of speculation. There may not have been any great delay, since the affluent merchant class was apparently keeping abreast of current styles by importing furniture. The "Dutch painted cupboard" entered in the same 1702 inventory as a "great black walnut cupboard" is a tantalizing reference.[111] Certainly New York did not lack painters in the late seventeenth and early eighteenth centuries.[112]

It has been seen that related styles of grisaille decoration, probably from the same school, are found on two types of American kasten. One is exemplified by catalogue number 5, which in its form, moldings, and use of oak seems to take its cues from seventeenth-century-style furniture. If it comes from New York City as presumed, the kast was very likely made no later than the early eighteenth century. Its earliest possible date is suggested by the painted perimeter molding on the doors, which reflects stylistic influences probably not felt in New York before the 1690s. The second category of kast, a Baroque type with a drawer in the base like figure 28, was made throughout the 1700s; however, the door construction of these grisaille pieces points to the early decades of the century.

On this basis, then, a possible range of dates between 1690 and 1730 is proposed for the group of five New York kasten with related decoration. The character of that decoration, still quite close to the Dutch tradition, is in keeping with the structural and stylistic evidence. The extent to which any of the other examples of grisaille painting represent a direct outgrowth of the presumed New York school or a variant tradition transferred from the Netherlands is still to be determined, as is an answer to the question of how much deeper into the eighteenth century any of them might date.

Notes

1. For a description, see Vernon S. Gunnion, "The Pennsylvania-German *Schrank*," *Antiques*, May 1983, pp. 1022–26.

2. Benno M. Forman, *American Seating Furniture, 1630–1730* (New York, 1988), p. 294.

3. J. Franklin Jameson, *Narratives of New Netherlands* (New York, 1909), p. 259.

4. See David S. Cohen, "How Dutch Were the Dutch of New Netherlands?" *New York History*, January 1981, pp. 52–53; and Thomas L. Purvis, "The National Origins of New Yorkers in 1790," *New York History*, April 1986, pp. 144–45.

5. Peter Kalm, *Travels in North America* (London, 1772), vol. 1, p. 210.

6. Joel Munsell, "Albany as Seen by Dr. Dwight," *Annals of Albany* 8 (1857), pp. 181–83.

7. Quoted in Schama, *Embarrassment of Riches*, p. 305. In 1537 the Italian architect Sebastiano Serlio (1475–1552) published the first book that illustrated the five classical orders. Two years later an edition was published in Antwerp. Thus architects, builders, and craftsmen in the Netherlands had access at an early date to the architectural standards of antiquity, although they preferred the free-form inventions of Mannerism.

8. Reinier Baarsen, "The Court Style in Holland," in Reinier Baarsen et al., *Courts and Colonies: The William and Mary Style in Holland, England, and America*, exh. cat., Cooper-Hewitt Museum (New York, 1988), p. 15.

9. See C. H. Box, *The Dutch Seaborne Empire* (New York and London, 1965).

10. Lunsingh Scheurleer, "Dutch and Their Homes," p. 25.

11. Collection of the Rijksmuseum, Amsterdam; reproduced in Helena Hayward, ed., *World Furniture, an Illustrated History* (New York, 1965), fig. 229.

12. Copies of the emblem books are difficult to locate; for reproductions of the illustrations, see Schama, *Embarrassment of Riches*, particularly figs. 186 and 224.

13. Ibid., p. 376.

14. *The Dutch Drawn to Life* (1665); quoted in Schama, *Embarrassment of Riches*, p. 375.

15. De Blainville, *Travels Through Holland*; see Schama, *Embarrassment of Riches*, p. 377.

16. Schama, *Embarrassment of Riches*, especially chapter 6, "Housewives and Hussies: Homeliness and Worldliness."

17. Observed by Gilbert T. Vincent in 1985; also, some discussion

of border-area kasten can be found in Wilhelm Elling, *Alte Möbel im Westmünsterland* (Vreden, 1984); and Dörte Becker, *Bäuerliche und bürgerliche Möbel aus dem Westmünsterland* (Münster, 1984).

18. When establishing the New Netherland colony, Dutch authorities complained about the difficulty of finding emigrants, since many native Dutch were content in their homeland. Settlers from Germany, France, Flanders, and Scandinavia were encouraged to join the colony. Because the Counter-Reformation was particularly successful in northwestern Germany during the late 17th century, many Protestants fled that area for North America.

19. *Collections of the New-York Historical Society for the Year 1895* (New York, 1896), p. 122.

20. *Collections of the New-York Historical Society for the Year 1897* (New York, 1898), p. 431.

21. *Collections of the New-York Historical Society for the Year 1896* (New York, 1897), p. 29.

22. Schama, *Embarrassment of Riches*, p. 379.

23. N. Hudson Moore, *The Old Furniture Book* (New York, 1935), p. 31.

24. Alice P. Kenney, *The Gansevoorts of Albany* (Syracuse, 1969), p. 152.

25. Joel Munsell, "Random Recollections," *Annals of Albany* 10 (1859), p. 191.

26. Joel Munsell, "Winterbotham's 'View of the United States of America,'" *Annals of Albany* 8 (1857), p. 191.

27. [Washington Irving], *A History of New York, from the Beginning of the World to the End of the Dutch Dynasty . . . by Diedrich Knickerbocker* ([1809]; 4th Amer. ed., New York, 1824), p. 185.

28. *Collections of the New-York Historical Society for the Year 1897* (New York, 1898), p. 437.

29. Ibid., p. 215.

30. Singleton, *Furniture of Our Forefathers*, p. 263.

31. Sold at Cater's Auction, West Berne, New York, May 1985.

32. *Collections of the New-York Historical Society for the Year 1893* (New York, 1894), p. 72. "Mr. Shaveltie" may refer to the New York joiner John (Jean) le Chevalier; see note 61 below.

33. *Collections of the New-York Historical Society for the Year 1896* (New York, 1897), p. 39.

34. For an example with geometric applied moldings and small central projections and a history of ownership in America (present location unknown) see Frances Clary Morse, *Furniture of the Olden Time* (New York, 1902), pp. 86–87, fig. 59; for an elaborate example with broad raised panels see Hayward, *World Furniture*, p. 73, fig. 231.

35. See, for example, Hayward, *World Furniture*, p. 53, fig. 158.

36. Illustrations of Dutch doors of the first half of the 17th century provided by J. Schipper; in the archives of the Department of American Decorative Arts, The Metropolitan Museum of Art (MMA).

37. The side panels of the kast shown in figs. 10–11 have triangular ebonized recesses at the top and bottom of their inner fields. Originally these may have held ebony insets like those on the sides of a two-stage kast with narrow *kussens* on the doors dated 1652 (*Antiek* 18 [October 1983], inside back cover).

38. See page 8. For examples of furniture see Elling, *Alte Möbel im Westmünsterland*, p. 122, fig. 92, and pp. 316–17, figs. 314–15.

39. In New England, fielded panels were exceptional before the 1690s, occurring earlier primarily on some Boston furniture; for example, Robert F. Trent, "The Chest of Drawers in America, 1635–1730, a Postscript," *Winterthur Portfolio* 20 (Spring 1985), p. 44, fig. 16 (single-field panels left plain); Helen Comstock, *American Furniture* (New York, 1962), fig. 64 (with an applied molding).

40. Exceptions include the wainscot chair at Yale University (Patricia E. Kane, *300 Years of American Seating Furniture* [Boston, 1976], pp. 29–30) and the one at the Connecticut Historical Society (Jonathan L. Fairbanks and Robert F. Trent, *New England Begins: The Seventeenth Century*, 3 vols. [Boston, 1982], no. 179; also, no. 171 for a chest possibly by a Dutch joiner).

41. A variation occurs on the large group of "Hadley" chests; see John T. Kirk, *American Furniture and the British Tradition to 1830* (New York 1982, p. 97).

42. In the 18th century in all the colonies a smaller, more rounded ovolo without a bead is frequently worked on the edges of the framing members of interior woodwork and some furniture, and is used on the framed sides of kasten cat. no. 6 and fig. 17.

43. Information on this usage from H. Zantkuyl and J. Schipper; correspondence in the archives of the Department of American Decorative Arts, MMA.

44. See drawings, sheets 12 and 15, Historic American Buildings Survey; Library of Congress, ref. no. Ulster County (56).

45. This profile also appears on English furniture and woodwork and is found in the 17th century in New England applied to joined furniture made or influenced by London-trained joiners (for example, Fairbanks and Trent, *New England Begins*, nos. 481, 482, 484).

46. See for example Lunsingh Scheurleer, "Dutch and Their Homes," p. 26, fig. 6.

47. See for example Trent, "Chest of Drawers," figs. 9, 13–18.

48. For an illustration of the desk see Baarsen et al., *Courts and Colonies*, p. 154, no. 103.

49. For Dutch houses see correspondence with H. Zantkuyl, archives of the Department of American Decorative Arts, MMA, and Marvin D. Schwartz, *The Jan Martense Schenck House* (New York: Brooklyn Museum, 1964), p. 23 fig. 13, p. 24, and p. 20 fig. 11 (an early view of New Amsterdam houses).

50. I. N. Phelps Stokes, *The Iconography of Manhattan Island, 1498–1909*, vol. 4 (New York, 1922), p. 157; translated differently in Singleton, *Dutch New York*, pp. 44–45.

51. The doors of New England joined cupboards are hinged with wood pins extending from the top and bottom door rails into the rails of the case.

52. On cat. no. 3 the leaves of the hinge are recessed into the outer edge of the door and case stiles for a short distance and then bend at a right angle to enter the mortise. Such hinges were used in the Netherlands from the beginning of the 17th century onward (correspondence with J. Schipper and H. Zantkuyl, archives of the Department of American Decorative Arts, MMA).

53. Failey, *Long Island Is My Nation*, pp. 36–37.

54. Stokes, *Iconography of Manhattan Island*, pp. 91, 93, 97 (for Hendricks); p. 94 (for English carpenters John Hubbesen [Hubbardson or Hubertson] and John Meris [Morris or Maurice]); pp. 95–96 (for Thomas Chambers). For Labatie see Paul R. Huey, "Archeological Evidence of Dutch Wooden Cellars and Perishable Wooden Structures at Seventeenth- and Eighteenth-Century Sites in the Upper Hudson Valley," in *New World Dutch Studies*, pp. 14, 17.

55. For published names of Long Island woodworkers see Failey, *Long Island Is My Nation*, Appendix I, pp. 222–93. The names of early craftsmen have been compiled by Neil Kamil of Brandeis University and will be made available in the catalogue of a future exhibition.

56. "The Burghers of New Amsterdam and the Freemen of New York, 1675–1866," in *Collections of the New-York Historical Society for 1885* (New York, 1886), pp. 20–23, 25.

57. Stokes, *Iconography of Manhattan Island*, p. 212.

58. Failey, *Long Island Is My Nation*, p. 289.

59. For contracts, see note 50 above and Henk J. Zantkuyl, "The Netherlands Town House: How and Why It Works," in *New World Dutch Studies*, pp. 150–56. For Dutch sheathing and doors see Henk J. Zantkuyl, "De houten huizen van Holysloot," *Bulletin van de Koninklijke Nederlandse Oudheidkundige Bond* 67 (1968), pp. 11–27, figs. 3 and 14; and information provided by J. Schipper, archives of the Department of American Decorative Arts, MMA.

60. Singleton, *Dutch New York*, pp. 83, 93, 99.

61. In 1675 a Jan Cauelier billed the City of New York for repairing the royal arms on the front of the city hall and for making a frame for it (Stokes, *Iconography of Manhattan Island*, p. 305). This must be the Jean le Chevalier who in 1700 was paid for carving work on the customhouse barge (ibid., p. 422) and appears as a joiner in the 1695

list of freemen ("Burghers of New Amsterdam," p. 58). For a 1663 reference to portrait painting by Henri Coutourier see Blackburn and Piwonka, *Remembrance of Patria*, p. 214.

62. Peter M. Kenny, "A Study of the Eighteenth-Century Grote Kast in Ulster County, New York," unpublished senior research paper, Cooperstown Graduate Program, SUNY Oneonta, 1984.

63. O'Donnell, "Grisaille Decorated *Kasten*," p. 1108; Singleton, *Furniture of Our Forefathers*, p. 245.

64. In addition to cat. nos. 6 and 8 and fig. 16, two unpainted American Baroque kasten with perimeter door moldings are known. One, from the Glen-Sanders family, is at the Schenectady County Historical Society, Schenectady, New York, and is illustrated in Colonial Williamsburg, Department of Collections, *The Glen-Sanders Collection from Scotia, New York* (Williamsburg, Va., 1966), p. 15. The second, illustrated in *Antiques*, June 1971, p. 895, is the only example with perimeter door moldings that has applied panels on the front stiles. Grisaille-painted kasten with perimeter door moldings are discussed in this essay, p. 29.

65. More research into Dutch immigration after the English takeover might reveal the names and birthplaces of provincial Dutch joiners who could have brought fully formed, vernacular Baroque kast designs to New York. Some recent German studies on provincial furniture from the German-Dutch border areas (see note 17 above) indicate that kasten similar in quality to the American Baroque examples were being made there as well.

66. Abraham Keteltas (ca. 1675–1744) and his brother Gerrit (1680–1746) were New York City merchants. By the early 19th century some of Gerrit's descendants had moved to Staten Island. In 1851 the contents of the home of John Keteltas, great-grandson of Gerrit, were noted: "In Mr. K's house are some fine specimens of old fashioned furniture, all of which are mentioned in the Inventories . . . the one called a 'Cubbard' (p. 166) is a very fine and massive wardrobe, of large size, and stately though plain appearance, resting on large balls. It is apparently of cherry wood." Recorded in "Anthon's Notes," *Proceedings of the Staten Island Institute of Arts and Sciences, Oct. 1929–May 1930*, vol. 5, part 1, pp. 102–3.

67. Ruth Piwonka, "New York Colonial Inventories: Dutch Interiors as a Measure of Cultural Change," in *New World Dutch Studies*, pp. 66–67, 74–76. The 1744 estate inventory of Abraham Keteltas in his account book, which is at the New-York Historical Society, lists "1 Old Bylsead [red gum] Cuperd" in a second-floor bedroom. If this is the kast in fig. 16, the reason for its knock-down design becomes clear.

68. The early use of mahogany in New York furniture is demonstrated by the mahogany applied panels on the front of a desk inscribed 1695 in the Metropolitan Museum (fig. 18). The panels are not of walnut and may be a variety of American mahogany (opinion rendered by R. Bruce Hoadley; see acc. file 44.47, Department of American Decorative Arts, MMA).

69. For two kasten with applied mahogany panels on the stiles, double-fielded door panels, and Kings County histories, see Maud E. Dilliard, *An Album of New Netherland* (New York, 1963), pl. 95, and *The City of New York, a History Illustrated from the Collections of the Museum of the City of New York* (New York, 1978), p. 35.

70. Failey, *Long Island Is My Nation*, pp. 124–25.

71. Both, Staten Island Historical Society; Seguine kast, acc. no. F1.53; Journeay kast (partially disassembled), unnumbered.

72. New Jersey State Museum, Trenton. New Jersey features are a large cyma recta profile in the architrave, applied diamonds behind the drawer pulls, a drawer opening sawn out of a single board rather than framed, and end-grain pins in the dovetail joints of the base that are less steeply pitched and have wider necks than is usual for Kings County kasten.

73. Failey, *Long Island Is My Nation*, p. 13.

74. The bolection moldings on the fireplace in the Hewlett Room from Woodbury, Long Island, now in the Metropolitan Museum (ca. 1740–60) have the same basic profile, although the ovolo and cavetto profiles are more deeply worked.

75. The carved feet on the 1622 Dutch kast shown in fig. 3 extend from front to back and serve as platforms on which the kast rests. Bernard D. Cotton of the Regional Furniture Society in England writes that he knows of no similar platform feet in English work (letter, April 5, 1990).

76. For Long Island double-paneled chests and the desk on frame see Failey, *Long Island Is My Nation*, pp. 104–8, 130, and Huyler Held, "Chests from Western Long Island," *Antiques*, January 1939, pp. 14–15.

77. In a list of Long Island woodworking craftsmen (Failey, *Long Island Is My Nation*, Appendix I), only about a dozen of the more than three hundred in Queens County had Dutch surnames. Failey (pp. 109–10) cites the ownership of kasten by Quaker families on the north shore of Queens County. The kast in fig. 20 seems entirely in keeping with the oft-cited Quaker maxim "Of the best sort but plain." A desk (Museum of the City of New York) from Flushing, another part of Queens County where Quakers settled among the Dutch, shows clear Quaker influence in its profusion of inlaid line-and-berry ornament. See Baarsen et al., *Courts and Colonies*, no. 103.

78. They included Jotham Wright (1708–?), a joiner from Oyster Bay, who also worked in Rye, New York; the "shop joiner" Ananias Brush, who went from Huntington, Long Island, to New Milford, Connecticut, in the 1770s; and several other carpenters from Queens County. See Failey, *Long Island Is My Nation*, Appendix I.

79. Many English settlers from Connecticut settled in Westchester County beginning in the late 17th century; presumably the Dutch spilled over into southern coastal Connecticut towns as well. For mixed Anglo-Dutch population in this area see Frederick W. Bogert, "Westchester's Unknown Dutch," *de Halve Maen* 51, no. 1 (Spring 1977), pp. 13–14.

80. The clothespress at Yale, which has interior fitments in the cupboard section typical of a Pennsylvania German *Schrank* as well as other German joinery features, is made with multipaneled doors and stiles and a range of drawers in the lower section, and has proportions much like those of cat. no. 15. It is illustrated in Gerald W. R. Ward, *American Case Furniture* (New Haven, 1988), pp. 392–94. Bernard D. Cotton has suggested a possible relationship between the multipaneled Connecticut kasten and some cupboard forms from the English-Welsh border areas.

81. The kast is illustrated in Norman F. Rice, *New York Furniture Before 1840* (Albany, 1962), p. 39.

82. In classical architecture the glyph appears in friezes of the Doric order where it is a vertically oriented device usually employed in groups of three. In the 16th century the glyph was transformed into an element of Mannerist design, used decoratively in both horizontal and vertical positions on the facades of case furniture.

83. See Stuart M. Blumin, *The Urban Threshold: Growth and Change in a Nineteenth-Century American Community* (Chicago and London, 1976), p. 35, where this homogeneity is attributed to intermarriage with the predominating Dutch and universal membership in the Dutch Reformed Church.

84. Policies established by the proprietor of the colony prohibited private ownership of farmland, allowing property to be owned only in the tiny village of Beverwyck. Many early settlers in the Esopus region maintained residences and owned property in both Rensselaerswyck and Ulster County; see Marc B. Fried, *The Early History of Kingston and Ulster County, N. Y.* (Marbletown and Kingston, New York, 1975), p. 150.

85. Helen W. Reynolds, *Dutch Houses in the Hudson Valley Before 1776* (New York, 1919), p. 178.

86. Elting family genealogy, typescript in the Haviland-Heidgerd Historical Collection at the Elting Memorial Library, New Paltz, New York. For the reference to Elting in the Flatbush town records see Failey, *Long Island Is My Nation*, Appendix I, p. 275; for Elting's bequest to his son Hendricus see Gustave Anjou, *Ulster County, New York, Probate Records* (New York, 1906), vol. 2, p. 131.

87. *New York Genealogical and Biographical Record* 74 (April 1943), pp. 59–61.

88. *Transcripts of Early County Records of New York State* (Albany: Historical Records Survey, 1939), p. 43.

89. J. H. Beers, *Commemorative Biographical Record of Ulster County, New York* (Chicago, 1896), p. 869.

90. Benno M. Forman, "German Influences in Pennsylvania Furniture," in *Arts of the Pennsylvania Germans* (New York and London, 1983), pp. 102–70.

91. A kast with a Bergen County history closely related to the signed Roelof Demarest example is owned by the Blauvelt-Demarest Foundation, River Edge, New Jersey; see Volk, "Dutch Kast and American Kas," pp. 107–17.

92. A Bergen County kast with a compass inlay very similar to figs. 26 and 43 and the signed Demarest example was offered at the Skinner Americana sale (Bolton, Mass.), October 27–28, 1989, lot no. 591, and is illustrated in the sale catalogue.

93. Inverted corners appear in the upper section of a Dutch door in the 1818 Vreeland house in Nordhoff, New Jersey. Scale drawings showing other details of the door, including profiles of its moldings, related to aspects of the door panels of Bergen County kasten are in Clifford C. Wendehack, "Early Dutch Houses of New Jersey," *White Pine Series of Architectural Monographs* 11, no. 3 (1925), pp. 11–17.

94. The MMA kast (O'Donnell, "Grisaille Decorated *Kasten*," p. 1110, fig. 5) originally had board feet like cat. no. 5 and in all probability a frieze drawer; it has been cut down and given a new top board. The kast in Gracie Mansion, New York City, which belongs to The Art Commission, City of New York, has had its back, top, bottom, shelves, and architrave and base moldings replaced (Firth Haring Fabend, "Two 'New' Eighteenth-Century Grisaille Kasten," *Clarion*, Spring/Summer 1981, pp. 44–49, figs. 1–3).

95. Fabend, "Two 'New' Grisaille Kasten," fig. 5. Probably the kast originally had an ovolo frieze molding on the sides as well as on the front.

96. The drawer of fig. 28 is dovetailed at the front and nailed at the back; its base is dovetailed in the manner of Kings County kasten (see page 20), but the end-grain pins do not have thin necks. On the kast at the Van Cortlandt House in the Bronx (O'Donnell, "Grisaille Decorated *Kasten*," p. 1108, fig. 1), the drawer is dovetailed front and back. The base, and that of the kast at the Monmouth County Historical Association (ibid., p. 1109, fig. 3), have the front and the backboards dovetailed to the sides, as was normally the case. The drawer of the latter kast is nailed.

97. Those doors either are joined or have an applied framework that simulates paneling. See for example Blackburn and Piwonka, *Remembrance of Patria*, pp. 268–69, and K. Boonenburg, "Beschilderde boerenmeubelen in het Zuiderzeegebied," *Bulletin van de Koninklijke Nederlandse Oudheidkundige Bond* 11 (1958), pp. 11–28, figs. 1–4, 9–13.

98. For the kast at Van Cortlandt Manor see O'Donnell, "Grisaille Decorated *Kasten*," p. 1111, fig. 6; for the MMA kast see Blackburn and Piwonka, *Remembrance of Patria*, p. 270.

99. Such ornament, used in England by the architect Inigo Jones (1573–1652), for example, is documented in Boston by an Ionic pilaster cap in stone, carved with a heavy festoon and two pendants of fruit, that survives from the facade of the Foster-Hutchinson house (1685–92); see Abbott Lowell Cummings, "The Domestic Architecture of Boston, 1660–1725," *Archives of American Art Journal* 9 (1971), p. 9, fig. 9. For related motifs on silver tankards from New York see Marshall Davidson, "Colonial Cherubim in Silver," *Antiques* 37 (April 1940), pp. 184–86.

100. De Jonge and Vogelsang, *Holländische Möbel und Raumkunst*, p. 151, fig. 220 (where it is described as a marriage cupboard and dated to about 1680). A table related to the cupboard's stand and dated about 1670 is shown in Hayward, *World Furniture*, p. 73, fig. 232.

101. Shirley Glubok, "The Dolls' House of Petronella de la Court," *Antiques* 137 (February 1990), pp. 493–94, 497, pl. 8.

102. For an example of painted woodwork see photographs provided by J. Schipper of the house in Haarlem rebuilt in 1648 for the Coymans family, in the archives of the Department of American Decorative Arts, MMA. For mid-17th-century grisailles on canvas, see Department of Paintings of the Rijksmuseum, *All the Paintings of the Rijksmuseum in Amsterdam* (Amsterdam, 1976), pp. 662–63.

103. For the kast in fig. 29 see G. J. Blees Kzn., "Oud-Zaansche volkskunst," *Het huis oud en nieuw* 12 (1914), p. 73, fig. 11. The piece is called a *kastje*, a diminutive indicating it was not large, and is dated about 1750 and described as formerly in the Friesian Mennonite Orphanage at Zaandam. The author is indebted to E. M. Klijn, curator at the Rijksmuseum voor Volkskunde, Openluchtmuseum, Arnhem, for this reference and photograph. The kast in fig. 30 was found by T. H. Lunsingh Scheurleer; it entered the collection of the Openluchtmuseum, Arnhem, in 1942 and was destroyed in 1944. The photograph was kindly provided by J. Schipper.

104. For the kast at the Zuiderzeemuseum in Enkhuizen see Blackburn and Piwonka, *Remembrance of Patria*, p. 267; for the one in the United States see *The Andy Warhol Collection, Americana and European and American Paintings, Drawings, and Prints*, Sotheby's, New York, April 29–30, 1988, lot 3189.

105. T. H. Lunsingh Scheurleer, *Van haardvuur tot beeldscherm* (Leiden, 1961), p. 98, mentions a 1698 contract in Amsterdam between a *witwerker* and a painter stipulating that each would work exclusively for the other and giving the price for painting different furniture forms; the highest price was for cupboards (*kabinetten*).

106. Blackburn and Piwonka, *Remembrance of Patria*, pp. 270–71.

107. *Architecture, peinture, et sculpture de la Maison de Ville d'Amsterdam* (Amsterdam, 1719), pl. 19.

108. For polychromed kasten see Boonenburg, "Beschilderde boerenmeubelen," figs. 2, 11; information and photographs on those kasten and on the use of brown and gray grisaille provided by J. Schipper in the archives of the Department of American Decorative Arts, MMA.

109. Blackburn and Piwonka, *Remembrance of Patria*, pp. 268–69; and Roderic H. Blackburn, "Dutch Decorative Painted Furniture since the 17th Century," *Decorator* 38 (Spring 1984), pp. 21–23.

110. In particular the grisailles by Jacob de Wit (1696–1754); see for example Rijksmuseum, *Paintings of the Rijksmuseum*, pp. 608–9.

111. Singleton, *Furniture of Our Forefathers*, p. 265.

112. Mary Black, "Early Colonial Painting of the New York Province," in Blackburn and Piwonka, *Remembrance of Patria*, pp. 209–55.

1. Joined Kast. Probably New York City or Vicinity

1650–1700

Red oak* and yellow pine*

H. 69 in. (175.3 cm); O.W. 53 1/8 in. (134.9 cm); O.D. 23 1/4 in. (59.1 cm)

Staten Island Historical Society, Richmondtown Restoration

◆

In this kast's panels with their rather high relief, solid oak is used to express the same bold outward movement seen on Dutch kasten with built-up beveled panels, where similarly the projection can be either long and narrow (fig. 4) or relatively wide (cat. no. 7). In very broad terms this piece recalls Dutch two-stage four-door *kussenkasten*, not only in its panels but also in the composition of its facade, a play of horizontal and vertical rectangles in which the frieze and the drawers in the base echo one another. Although the sides of most kasten are treated as secondary surfaces, the panels on the sides of this oak kast are design elements as prominent as those on the front (fig. 31), another feature reminiscent of some *kussenkasten* (see cat. no. 7).

The joined oak kast, however, does not display the same level of workmanship as its Dutch prototypes. There are substantial design differences as well. These may stem from a misunderstanding of the sources; from other, non-Dutch European influences; or from individual idiosyncrasy. Unlike four-door Dutch kasten, this example is made in one piece, with only a slight variation in height between its upper and lower sections. The facade lacks the broad stiles on both sides and between the doors which usually serve as pilasters extending upward from the bottom of the case. Rather, inconspicuous narrow corner posts supply the structural support, while the visible vertical emphasis usually furnished by the stiles is here provided by panels at either side, but only at the level of the doors. Consequently the kast does not have a strong architectural presence. This impression is no doubt reinforced by the loss of several moldings. On the sides, two at the top and two at the bottom are missing, and on the front the lower base molding has been lost. It is also possible that the cornice was reduced.

31. Detail, left side of catalogue number 1

The kast's panels, including those on the doors, are each worked from a single oak board. The drawer fronts are unusual in that they are worked like panels and thus are thin at the edges; this explains the presence of a slat running inside the bottom of each drawer front. The front is nailed to the slat as well as to the drawer sides, and the slat also provides a surface to which the bottom boards are nailed in front. The drawers run on the drawer bottoms, each on two supports let into the front and rear rails. The interior of the upper cupboard has a vertical partition and a high narrow shelf on either side (now replaced). The lower cupboard has no shelf or division. Pine is used only for the sides and back of one of the drawers.

The kast has a tradition of ownership in the Christophel, later Christopher, family of Staten Island, and was used in the house on Willowbrook Road that was acquired by Joseph Christopher between 1761 and 1764. In 1975 the house was moved to Richmondtown Restoration. Hans Christophel was one of the original petitioners who established the first permanent white settlement on Staten Island in 1661. He moved to Brooklyn, but by 1681 another Hans Christophel, possibly his son, was settled on Staten Island.

---

*Woods marked with an asterisk have been identified by microanalysis.

The presence of red oak in a piece of 17th-century furniture is considered an indication of American manufacture. See Forman, *American Furniture*, pp. 25–26.

2. Joined Kast. Probably New York City or Vicinity

1650–1700

White* and red oak*

H. 58 ⅜ in. (148.3 cm); O.W. 53 ⅜ in. (135.6 cm); O.D. 21 ¾ in. (55.3 cm)

Courtesy, Henry Francis du Pont Winterthur Museum

◆

Although this kast is built on a modest scale, it does not lack stature. With its doors flanked and divided by substantial stiles simulating pilasters, it has a solid architectonic presence. However, the drawer and the base from the floor to just above the bottom molding did not survive, and their reconstruction is perforce conjectural. Therefore, what the full original impact of this kast was cannot be known.

The kast's door panels, unlike those of the other oak examples, do not aim at high relief. Each presents a broad flat expanse in its upper field with just a narrow border to indicate the lower field. They are similar in effect to the wide door panels that are part of the Amsterdam woodwork shown in figure 7. The stiles and rails of the Dutch woodwork have rectangular recesses whose counterparts on the kast are the broad sunken band on the center door rails and the narrower pair on the side rails. Similar bands are worked into the center rail and uprights on the sides of the Dutch kast in figures 10–11. Recessed areas, rather than projecting elements, create much of the surface interest on this kast's facade.

The panels on the stiles create a rhythm of upward visual movement in counterpoint to the equal-height panels of the doors and the strong horizontal of the band in the door rails. The stile pattern of two shorter panels below a taller one is highly unusual on a two-door kast, although a similar rhythm is frequently seen in the paneling of four-door examples (fig. 3), and may be the source of this feature. The panels on the front stiles, like those on catalogue number 3 and figure 10, are actually simulated. They were formed by recessing the center of the stile along its full length and working a molding (here a small cyma) on the edge of the recess. Then insets edged top and bottom with the same molding were inserted to divide the recess into smaller units.

32. Detail, shelf on interior of catalogue number 2

The oak used in the kast is of narrow width throughout, the panels each being made of two boards. As in most joined American work, the oak was riven rather than sawn. Evidence of the tearing of wood that occurs during riving is retained on the boards of the back. They have the typical wedge-shaped center piece and fit into grooves in the stiles and top rail and are nailed to the other rails. The orientation of the rear stiles, whose wider face is toward the side of the case, is unusual. In the interior, only the upper of the two original shelves remains (fig. 32). Other losses, including the right cornice and upper base moldings, the insets on the center stile, and the left board of the top, have been replaced.

In all probability this kast came from the estate of a member of the Bulmer family in Chester, New York. There were Bulmers in Chester and nearby Paterson, New Jersey, from about 1830 on, and in the eighteenth century in Somerset County, New Jersey. A direct link to the seventeenth century is yet to be established. However, in the eighteenth century at least two Bulmers/Bolmers married members of the Wiltsie/Willson family, whose progenitor in America had settled in Newtown (Queens County), Long Island, by 1669; members of that family moved to Somerset County shortly after 1700.[1]

1. Genealogical data compiled by Leslie P. Symington and now in the archives of the Department of American Decorative Arts, MMA.

3. Joined Kast. Probably New York City or Vicinity

1650–1700

White* and red oak,* painted

H. 70 in. (177.8 cm); O.W. 67 in. (170.2 cm); O.D. 25 in. (63.5 cm)

The Metropolitan Museum of Art, Gift of Millia Davenport, 1988 (1988.21)

◆

The kast is distinctive not only because of its arresting painted decoration but also because it represents a variation on the usual two-door format. It lacks the drawer normally below the cupboard section and also the center stile, identical to the side front stiles, that characteristically is attached to the right door. Consequently the facade does not incorporate the three dominant verticals that typically flank and divide a kast's front. Instead, the horizontality of the massive solid oak cornice and impressive base molding is counterbalanced by a composite of numerous vertical elements: the stiles and tall narrow panels of the doors and the front stiles of the case. The front stiles do not stand out as strongly as is usually the case because their panels follow the same rhythm as those on the doors. A recessed band, similar to those on the center rails of catalogue number 2, is worked on the face of the framing members of the doors. Thus there is a play back and forth between two planes on those framing members as well as on the case stiles with their recessed panels, and in addition there is the outward projection of the double-fielded panels. Therefore the facade does not lack visual interest, even discounting the striking marbleized surface that accentuates the panels and their narrow central fields and adds to the composition the elements of color and of contrast between lighter and darker areas.

The paint is applied in large free repetitive swirls to suggest, but not imitate, the appearance of variegated stone, red over white on the panels and cornice and black over blue-gray on the stiles and rails. Oak furniture was not usually painted over the entire surface. Whether this decoration was part of the original design or was added a little later is a question that has not been resolved. There is little with which to compare the decoration stylistically. Painting in this general manner seems to have been in use over a long period of time: it is found on an English piece dated 1628 and on New England grained furniture of the late seventeenth and early eighteenth centuries.[1] Painted decoration with related graining, although following a less regular pattern, occurs on a door from a mid-eighteenth-century house in New Jersey.[2] The pigments used on the kast—lead white and a carbon black, as on catalogue number 5, and red lead—were already available well before the earliest possible date for the kast.[3] On the other hand, the colors blue-gray and red were often applied to the woodwork of houses in Dutch cultural areas of the Hudson Valley quite far into the eighteenth century.[4]

This kast, as large as the three-part example that is catalogue number 4, is built in one piece and cannot easily be moved. No doubt because of the kast's cumbersome size and weight, the top was at one time sawed off below the cornice. (The top is now attached by means of metal plates screwed to the stiles.) The feet have been almost entirely replaced; the stubs that survived made it clear that originally the feet were extensions of the molded stiles. On the interior, the kast has lost its shelves, but the rear shelf rails and nail holes in the front stiles where front shelf rails were attached indicate that once there were two full shelves made of transverse boards. There is also evidence that a vertical partition divided the space above the top shelf.

Nothing is known of the kast's history before 1934, when it was published as in the collection of Mrs. Sara M. Sanders, of Closter (Bergen County), New Jersey.[5]

1. For the English example see John T. Kirk, *American Furniture and the British Tradition to 1830* (New York, 1982), pp. 68–69; for an American example see *American Antiques from Israel Sack Collection*, vol. 6 (Washington, D.C., 1979), pp. 1592–93.

2. Blackburn and Piwonka, *Remembrance of Patria*, pp. 28, 272–73.

3. R. D. Harley, *Artists' Pigments c. 1600–1835*, 2nd ed. (London, 1982), pp. 123, 159, 166–67.

4. Blackburn and Piwonka, *Remembrance of Patria*, pp. 131, 166.

5. Homer Eaton Keyes, "Identifying Traits in New York Furniture," *Antiques* 26 (October 1934), p. 144.

4. Joined Kast. Probably New York City or Vicinity

1675–1700

Red oak* and walnut

H. 67 ¼ in. (170.8 cm); O.W. 66 ¼ in. (168.3 cm); O.D. 28 ¼ in. (71.8 cm)

The Art Institute of Chicago, Sanford Fund

◆

With its three-part construction, ball front feet, and design that is clearly of architectural inspiration, this oak kast, of the four examples, comes closest to Dutch prototypes. Its top is an entablature nearly identical to the one in the de Passe design (fig. 4), with an oversize ovolo in the frieze, and even including the square plaques which serve as capitals to the pilaster-like stiles below them. The base with its drawer supports the whole structure. Details like the concealed pivot hinges and the now-missing sliding glyph to hide the keyhole express the same concern for a clean architectural facade as that manifest in Dutch kasten.

The facade, with its four identical square panels, is a well-ordered symmetrical composition punctuated by strongly beveled appliqués in solid walnut. These replicate with simple means the dramatic effect created by the structurally more complex built-up projecting panels on Dutch kasten (cat. no. 7, fig. 4). The full impact of those walnut appliqués, which because of their different color must originally have stood out against the oak, has regrettably been lost; at one time the surface of the kast must have been treated, and it is now a fairly uniform warm brown. Although the contrast would not be as strong as that of the ebony veneers found on Dutch oak examples like figure 10, the intent was doubtless the same.

33. Back of catalogue number 4

The design of this kast, while relatively forward-looking, does not go so far as to adopt the single-panel door scheme characteristic of two-door Dutch kasten. It is still built entirely in the joined oak tradition, with its doors formed of more than one panel and each panel made up of two narrow boards. On the other hand, the stiles are no longer articulated by simulated panels recessed in the solid wood, as they are on catalogue numbers 2 and 3, but by applied elements as is typical of American kasten of the eighteenth century.

The interior of the kast is remarkably intact. Though the narrow topmost shelf is missing, the piece retains its two full shelves; a shallow drawer is hung under the upper one. Such drawers are found both in Dutch and American Baroque pieces. Both this drawer and the one in the base, which has a walnut* backboard, are side hung and of nailed construction. The drawer bottoms, like the top, the shelves, and the bottom of the cupboard section, are made from numerous narrow front-to-back tongue-and-groove boards. Tenons connect the rails of the kast's three structural units to hold them in place, as is the case in catalogue number 7, for instance, but not in American eighteenth-century pieces. With all this kast's relative refinements, the quick and easy manner in which the back was constructed comes as something of a surprise. It is simply made of overlapped clapboards nailed to the back rails, with the piece at either extremity fitting into a groove in the stiles (fig. 33).

This kast, acquired by the Art Institute of Chicago in 1949, was until recent years the only American oak kast generally known. Its history, unfortunately, goes no further than dealers.

5. Grisaille-Painted Kast. Probably New York City

1690–1720

Yellow poplar,* red oak,* and eastern white pine,* painted

H. 61 ½ in. (156.2 cm); O.W. 60 ⅜ in. (153.4 cm); O.D. 23 in. (58.4 cm)

The Metropolitan Museum of Art, Rogers Fund, 1909 (09.175)

◆

This kast and the closely related example at Gracie Mansion in New York City can be considered the earliest of the American grisaille pieces by virtue of their form and particularly the character of their decoration. The painting on this kast is the closest, all told, to the known Dutch examples, both in its motifs and in the degree of illusionism it achieves. As on the Dutch grisaille kast shown in figure 29, the niche is painted with a section of wall below that carries a decorative panel. The niche appears deep enough to believably contain a pendant in the round, and that pendant is secured to a keystone, an architectural element prominently displayed in figure 29. This is the only American kast with a clear replication of the acanthus motif that occurs on the friezes of all the Dutch grisaille examples.[1] One element of its decoration, however, the perimeter molding painted on the doors, has no known Dutch precedent, and may be an American innovation. The impressive, rich surface was achieved by simple means: painting the plain boards of the kast with lead white and carbon black over a blue-gray ground coat that is a mixture of the two pigments.

The salient structural feature of the kast is a bold ovolo, containing a drawer, in the frieze area; a prominent ovolo base molding balances the nearly square composition. The kast's top, recalling the three-part division of an entablature, is similar to that of catalogue number 4, but the overall design of the piece may owe more to Dutch board kasten like figure 29. However, the profile of the base molding is virtually identical to that of New York oak kasten (cat. nos. 3, 4) and does not seem to correspond closely to the base moldings of Dutch painted examples that have been published. Certainly the utilization of oak as a secondary wood in a piece of inexpensive board construction must be a New World phenomenon; in the Netherlands, oak was scarce by the late seventeenth century.

34. Detail, back of catalogue number 5

The riven oak clapboards, overlapped and nailed, that form the back of this kast (fig. 34) are an unusual and distinctive structural feature, seen in one other grisaille example (MMA 23.171) and in catalogue number 4. A single such clapboard constitutes the back of the drawer and another the narrow top shelf inside the cupboard. Otherwise the kast is made of broad sawn yellow poplar boards. It is entirely of nailed construction. Most joints are simply butted, but the sides are let into grooves in the top and the bottom and two full shelves into grooves in the sides. Each door is a single thick board, strengthened on the interior by two battens that are scribed with a grid of rectangles to guide the placement of the nails. Similar scribing occurs on the battens of two related kasten (MMA 23.171 and the Gracie Mansion kast) and has also been found on a pair of house shutters,[2] suggesting this was a traditional, not merely an individual, manner of working.

An ovolo-and-bead molding, a hallmark of the joined oak kasten, is run on the edges of the door battens. This profile and the cyma used on the center stile and the bottom of the architrave seem to have been formed by a molding plane. However, the edge of the top board, the convex frieze, the top element of the architrave (fig. 34), and the ovolo of the base molding were all shaped by a flat or hollow plane. The kast has minor replacements and repairs. The pull missing from the center of the drawer was probably an iron ring attached by means of a strap cotter pin through a shaped plate like the one on the kast at Gracie Mansion.

1. For the kast in Gracie Mansion, see essay note 94. The kast's frieze drawer has a rosette in the center and a winged cherub's head at either end.

2. Blackburn and Piwonka, *Remembrance of Patria*, p. 131.

6. Kast. Probably New York City

1690–1720

H. 77 in. (195.6 cm); O.W. 79 1/2 in. (201.9 cm); O.D. 28 3/8 in. (72.1 cm)

Red gum and pine[1]

Private collection

◆

This important example[2] is among the most stylish American Baroque kasten made. It has much in common with Dutch Baroque kasten of the period 1675–1700 (figs. 8, 35), particularly its applied perimeter door moldings and the broad swaths of mitered veneer that surround and isolate the fields in the center of the doors. That the kast is nonetheless a provincial work is apparent from its construction out of solid native red gum (even the thick veneer on the door panels) and its lack of applied carving. Less obvious details that also betray the kast's humbler origins are the standard joiner's frame-and-panel doors that lie beneath the applied moldings and veneer. On Dutch Baroque kasten like the one shown in figure 35, these parts are applied instead to solid board substructures, which are veneered on the backs as well.

This kast is the more elaborate of two examples with perimeter-molded doors that originally stood in a house belonging to the Glen-Sanders family of Scotia, New York. (The second, simpler, example, now at the Schenectady County Historical Society, lacks the central field and mitered veneers on the doors.) John Sanders (1714–1782) and Deborah Glen (1721–1793) inherited the house after they were married in 1739,[3] but because the style and construction of the kast suggest an early date of manufacture, its original owners were probably of the previous generation. Sanders' parents, Barent Sanders and Maria Wendel, were married in 1704; Glen's parents, Jacob Glen and Sara Wendel, were married in 1717. Maria and Sara Wendel were, respectively, daughter and granddaughter of the successful Albany fur trader Evert Jansen Wendel (1617–1709), who had many wide-ranging business connections. Perhaps this kast was purchased in New York City for Maria and served as the model for the simpler Glen-Sanders family kast. It is likely that an American kast as closely linked as this one is to high-style Dutch Baroque kast design was made in New York City.

The unusually small cornice of this three-part kast is original and unaltered, and resembles the one on an early, mahogany kast here attributed to a New York City maker (fig. 17). A treasured family possession for many years, catalogue number 6 underwent a thoroughgoing restoration in the 1920s, during which its entire back was replaced and its surface given a coat of thick, opaque varnish.[4]

35. Kast, Dutch, 1675–1700. Walnut veneer on oak, H. 87 in. (221 cm). This kast descended in the Beekman family of New York City and was probably imported from the Netherlands before 1700. The New-York Historical Society

1. Unless otherwise noted, woods have been identified by eye. Secondary woods are always named last.

2. Joseph Downs recognized this kast as a particularly important and early American Baroque example when he selected it for the first major loan exhibition of New York furniture in 1934 (see *A Loan Exhibition of New York State Furniture*, exh. cat., The Metropolitan Museum of Art (New York, 1934), p. 1.

3. See Colonial Williamsburg, Department of Collections, *The Glen-Sanders Collection from Scotia, New York* (Williamsburg, Va., 1966), for an illustration of the second kast and for a brief history and partial listing of the contents of the house, which remained in the family's possession until the mid-20th century. In the 19th century this kast was in use by the Ten Broeck family of Clermont, Columbia County, New York; see the MMA exhibition catalogue cited in note 2.

4. Information on the kast's restoration was provided by Miss Helen MyndERSE, the last descendant of the Glen-Sanders family to own the piece.

7. *Kussenkast.* Northern Provinces of the Netherlands

1650–90

Rosewood and ebony veneers over oak and pine

H. 83 in. (210.8 cm); O.W. 75 1/2 in. (191.8 cm); O.D. 25 5/8 in. (65.1 cm)

Lent by The Brooklyn Museum, Gift of Miss Mary van Kleeck in memory of Charles M. van Kleeck

◆

The most elaborate kasten in colonial New York were undoubtedly the veneered and carved examples imported from the Netherlands. The full Baroque design of this example, with two large doors, engaged columns, a monumental classical cornice, and large turned feet, was established in the cabinetmaking centers of the province of Holland, particularly Amsterdam, by the middle of the seventeenth century. A kast very similar to catalogue number 7 dominates a Dutch interior in the painting by Pieter de Hooch shown in figure 36. The greatly extended door and side panels, which reminded the Dutch of cushions, gave rise to the homely domestic term *kussenkast* for these opulent pieces of furniture.

Seven Dutch kasten in the Baroque style with seventeenth- and eighteenth-century New York histories are known today. Two are *kussenkasten.*[1] One descended in the Elting family of Kingston and according to tradition was imported in 1677; it is now located at Washington's Headquarters State Historic Site, Newburgh, New York. The example illustrated here descended from François Rombouts, a native of Hasselt near Liège, who immigrated to New York City and became a successful merchant. In 1674 he built an opulent mansion on Broadway[2] and in 1679 he was appointed mayor. His 1691/2 inventory lists five cupboards, an indication of considerable wealth; this *kussenkast* is probably the "holland Cubbert furnished with Earton ware and Parslin."[3]

36. Pieter de Hooch (Dutch, 1629–after 1684), *Interior with Figures.* Oil on canvas. The Metropolitan Museum of Art, Robert Lehman Collection, 1975 (1975.1.144). Note the contrasting veneers of rosewood and ebony on the *kussenkast* in the background, and the decorative display of porcelain and glass on its top.

The Rombouts *kussenkast* is built in three parts, each fitting onto vertical tenons. The structure is almost entirely oak, with the cornice, panels, and large moldings built up of multiple strips and blocks. The surface is covered with rosewood and ebony veneers. The turned feet are replacements and originally may have resembled the plain ball feet on the kast in the de Hooch painting. The distinctive waved molding was made mechanically by a technique invented in Nuremberg about 1600. Molding of this type became a popular embellishment for looking glasses and picture frames as well as case pieces, and its use had spread rapidly through Germany and into the Netherlands by the 1620s. By the end of the century the decorative motif was out of vogue and no longer in use.[4]

---

1. The other five include figure 35; examples from the Livingston and Van Rensselaer families (Blackburn and Piwonka, *Remembrance of Patria,* p. 176, and Singleton, *Furniture of Our Forefathers,* p. 234); and two from the Staats family, one at the Van Cortland House in the Bronx, the other in a private collection in Philadelphia.

2. I. N. Phelps Stokes, *The Iconography of Manhattan Island 1498–1909,* vol. 2 (New York, 1916), p. 222.

3. O'Donnell, "Grisaille Decorated *Kasten,*" p. 1108.

4. Volker Jutzi and Peter Ringger, "Die Wellenleiste und ihr maschinelle Herstellung," *Maltechnik* 2 (April 1986), pp. 34–62.

8. Kast. Kings County, New York, or New York City

1700–1730

Red gum, yellow poplar, and pine

H. 83 in. (210.8 cm); O.W. 79 ¼ in. (201.3 cm); O.D. 30 ¾ in. (78.1 cm)

Lent by The Brooklyn Museum, Gift of Mrs. Gertrude Cortelyou Bunn

◆

This kast is one of the rare American Baroque examples with perimeter door moldings and is the only surviving example of its type. Two other kasten probably by the same maker are known, but these have standard door frames and applied panels instead of pilasters on the stiles; one is shown in figure 37.[1]

The kast has a history of ownership in the Cortelyou, Bergen, Lefferts, Van Brunt, and Couwenhoven families of Brooklyn and was donated to the Brooklyn Museum in 1921. Its family history and its similarity in a number of ways to the far more common type of Kings County kast with applied mahogany panels on the stiles, such as catalogue number 9, suggest that this piece was made in Brooklyn or one of the other original Dutch towns on the western end of Long Island. It shares with those kasten the use of fussy, small-scale molding profiles in the architrave; a characteristic profile for the upper and lower base moldings; a base unit in which the front is dovetailed to the sides and the sides to the back; and a drawer that has corner joints dovetailed at the front and nailed at the back and an inner strut let into the drawer front with a sliding dovetail joint and butted and nailed to the back.

37. Kast, New York City or Kings County, New York, 1710–40. Red gum and pine, H. 79 ¼ in. (201.3 cm). Monmouth County Historical Association, Freehold, New Jersey, Gift of J. Campbell Henry

The construction of this kast's perimeter-molded doors is highly unusual and quite complicated. Instead of the perimeter moldings being applied to flat board substructures as in Dutch Baroque examples, or even to a standard joiner's frame-and-panel door as in catalogue number 6, here the deep cavetto profiles are worked in the solid on the extra-thick stiles and rails. On the back of the doors the stiles and rails come together at right angles as might be expected, but on the front they come together in a miter joint. This is accomplished by cutting the front shoulder of the rail tenon on a forty-five-degree angle and relieving the stile on a matching angle to accept it. Wood pegs are inserted through the joint and are visible on the face side. It is little wonder that only one kast of this particular design survives, given the complex, almost experimental nature of its joinery. The effect of the door panel design is quite dramatic, however, making this perhaps the most exciting of all American Baroque kasten.

Perimeter door moldings are features found on late-seventeenth-century Dutch Baroque kasten, as are other elements of this kast's design: applied rectangular panels behind the drawer pulls and pilasters on the front stiles, which here are so thin and sticklike that they could never give the illusion of bearing the weight of the massive cornice. The kast is built in three parts and has frame-and-panel sides on the cupboard section, a dovetailed base unit, and a dovetailed box substructure in the cornice.

1. The other belongs to the Huguenot Historical Society in New Paltz, New York, and is on display in the Terwilliger House.

9. Kast. Probably Kings County, New York

1710–40

Red gum, mahogany, and yellow poplar

H. 77 1/2 in. (196.9 cm); O.W. 72 1/2 in. (184.2 cm); O.D. 27 1/2 in. (69.9 cm)

Columbia County Historical Society, Kinderhook, New York

◆

Over fifty kasten are known having the distinctive design of this example, with applied mahogany panels on the front stiles. However, only a handful of them, including this kast, have been found in the central and upper Hudson River Valley. The greatest number that have family histories come from Kings County on western Long Island, Staten Island, and central New Jersey, and probably the kast design was endemic to those areas.

This kast was acquired in the late 1960s by the Columbia County Historical Society because it may have been owned by the Van Alen family and thus used in the Van Alen house in Kinderhook, New York, where it is now usually on display. The house was built in 1737 by Luykas Van Alen (ca. 1682–ca. 1762); however, there is no firm evidence linking him to the kast.

38. Detail of cornice and right stile of catalogue number 9, showing the complex architrave and glyph molding profiles typical of the Kings County school

The dating of Kings County kasten is greatly facilitated by their consistent use of brass English-style keyhole escutcheons which changed regularly over the course of time, going from William-and-Mary style designs like the one on this kast to pierced Rococo and oval Neoclassical designs in the later eighteenth century (by that time matching brass handles were also used on the drawer). The makers of these kasten in all likelihood purchased their furniture hardware from merchants in nearby New York City, who kept a fresh stock of the latest styles, imported from English manufacturers.

This kast appears to retain its original, thin, pigmented varnish finish and has a decidedly reddish cast. The characteristic Kings County use of mahogany in conjunction with red gum, the primary wood, is intriguing. The mahogany is in applied panels, where it was not intended as a contrast but instead served as a rich highlight of the more expensive imported wood that the red-hued native gumwood imitated. (A striped figure something like that of mahogany is obtained by sawing red gum radially; most Kings County kasten are made of red gum milled this way.[1])

The kast is constructed in two parts, with the cornice attached to the cupboard section and a separate dovetailed base unit having a drawer opening framed by an upper and lower rail and two filler pieces between the rails at the ends. The cupboard section has board sides and vertical tongue-and-groove backboards. The drawer has channeled sides that run on guides attached inside the base, and is constructed like the drawer of catalogue number 8. Inside the kast there is a shallow underhung drawer beneath the second shelf, a feature found in most Kings County kasten and in Dutch Baroque kasten, including the example in catalogue number 7, although its original purpose is unknown.

1. F. Lewis Hinckley, *Directory of the Historic Cabinet Woods* (New York, 1960), p. 58.

10. Kast. Kingston, New York

1700–1730

Attributed to the Elting-Beekman Shops

Red gum, yellow poplar, and pine

H. 81 in. (205.7 cm); O.W. 78 in. (198.1 cm); O.D. 30 in. (76.2 cm)

Hill-Hold Museum, Campbell Hall, New York

◆

Several features of this kast point to a date of manufacture early in the eighteenth century, and also indicate that the Elting-Beekman group of makers worked with a careful eye toward late-seventeenth-century Dutch Baroque kasten and even older Dutch designs. The kast is half a foot taller than most Ulster County examples and has a huge jutting cornice. Its doors have projecting, heavily built-up panels with recessed central fields, as shown in figure 24, a (in this instance the fields were resawn from a single board and book-matched), which serve as a counterpoint to the massive cornice. These elements give the kast something of the visual complexity and play of light and shadow that characterize its more sophisticated Dutch Baroque counterparts. Other design features that relate this kast to the Dutch kasten are the applied fields on its frame-and-panel sides (compare fig. 8) and the applied rectangular panels behind the drawer pulls (compare fig. 35). The applied pilasters on the front stiles may derive from the flat pilasters with applied carving on Dutch Baroque examples like figure 8. However, the use on this kast of a horizontal molding midway on the pilasters (on the center pilaster it covers the keyhole) may hearken back further to Dutch classicist design; note the ring on the column in the 1642 de Passe design (fig. 4). The same design carries moldings which seem near prototypes for the astragal-profile architrave and heavy ovolo base moldings on this kast. The ovolo-and-bead profile found on all the American oak kasten appears here as part of the applied bolection moldings on the door frames (fig. 39). Only in Ulster County does this older profile occur in Baroque-style kasten.

39. Detail of door of catalogue number 10 showing separate applied bevels, typical of early kasten from the Elting-Beekman shops. (See fig. 24, a.)

This kast and those in the two entries that follow are all similarly assembled. The kast is constructed in three sections. The front and back of the base unit are dovetailed to the sides, and the drawer opening in the front is framed of four pieces rather than sawn out of a solid board. The front feet of this kast appear to be original but have been removed at least once. The back feet are replacements and were originally simple posts. The dovetailed drawer with its channeled side is shown in figure 23. The cupboard section has frame-and-panel sides and vertical, tongue-and-groove backboards that are nailed into rebates at the back edges of the sides and attached to the back edges of the interior shelves with wooden pegs. Surmounting the dovetailed box substructure of the cornice are flat boards that are beveled where they adjoin the cornice molding, which is set at approximately a forty-five-degree angle.

When acquired by Hill-Hold Museum, the kast had a traditional history of ownership in the Jansen family of the Bruynswick area of southern Ulster County. The Jansens can be traced to Kingston as early as 1663. Some of them had moved into southern Ulster County by the 1720s, including the Thomas Jansen who built a stone house there in 1727.[1]

1. The history of the kast was given by Mrs. Helen Bell to the curator of Hill-Hold when she donated the kast to the museum. The Jansen house is illustrated in Helen Wilkinson Reynolds, *Dutch Houses in the Hudson Valley Before 1776* (New York, 1929), pl. 77.

11. Kast. Kingston, New York

1700–1730

Attributed to the Elting-Beekman Shops

Red gum, walnut, yellow poplar, and pine

H. 74 in. (188 cm); O.W. 76 in. (193 cm); O.D. 27 3/8 in. (69.5 cm)

Collection of Dr. George Bushnell

◆

This kast represents a second type designed by the Elting-Beekman group of makers—judging from the number of surviving examples, the most popular—and features applied panels and glyphs on the front stiles rather than pilasters with mid-moldings. Its frame-and-panel sides point to an early date of manufacture. Like catalogue number 10 it is an intriguing blend of elements echoing late-seventeenth-century Dutch Baroque kasten, American joined oak examples, and Dutch classicist kast design of the mid-seventeenth century.

40. Detail of door of catalogue number 11. Note the patch inset in the top bevel of the panel, replacing wood removed when the central field was plowed out with a plane. (See fig. 24, b.)

Dutch Baroque examples of about 1675–1700 seem the obvious model for the turned front feet of this kast, with its raised mounds rising out of flattened balls, and for the profile of its architrave molding, a wide fascia surmounted by a cavetto (figs. 8, 35). The same architrave is found in larger scale and with rich applied carving on the Dutch Baroque kasten. The door panels are shorthand versions of the complicated built-up variety used in catalogue number 10 and are formed by fielding the panel from a solid board and plowing out the center to create the recessed central field (figs. 40, 24, b). These panels have less Baroque vigor than the built-up type and probably were developed as a labor-saving technique, but they work well in a smaller kast, as does the slightly scaled-down cornice, very similar to the one on the Jansen kast but without the large central ovolo.

The flattened ovolo-and-bead molding profile familiar from American oak kasten appears in the applied bolection molding on the door frame, but here the ovolo is expanded slightly (fig. 40). The lower base molding combines a narrow fascia with a cavetto and an ogee above (fig. 22). The ogee, similarly expanded, bears comparison with the one at the top of the lower base molding on the oak kast catalogue number 4 (both are illustrated in Appendix D). This entry and catalogue number 4 also share the use of applied walnut glyphs. Those on the oak kast are overtly Mannerist in their massive scale; those on this later Ulster County example, although much smaller in scale, closely resemble in profile the large vertical one in de Passe's 1642 engraving (fig. 4).

According to the current owner of the kast, it descended in the La Montagne, Bevier, and Van Gaasbeck families of Ulster County and was discovered in the basement of the Van Leuven house on Wall Street in Kingston.

12. Kast. Kingston, New York

1780–1800

Attributed to the Elting-Beekman Shops

Red gum, sycamore, and pine

H. 73 3/8 in. (186.4 cm); O.W. 67 3/4 in. (172 cm); O.D. 22 3/8 in. (56.8 cm)

Collection of Mr. and Mrs. Richard R. Hasbrouck

◆

Not only is this kast still in the possession of the family who originally owned it, but, remarkably, it is still in use in the eighteenth-century house in New Paltz, New York, where it has always stood. The kast's first owner was probably Jacob J. Hasbrouck (1767–1850), whose father, Major Jacob Hasbrouck (1727–1806), is described as the builder of the oldest section of the house. Jacob J. lived in his father's house even after his two marriages, first to Margaret Hardenbergh (1776–1796) in 1793 and then to Ann Dubois (1777–1854) in 1799. A kast was frequently part of a woman's dowry, and this one probably came into the family on the occasion of one of these unions.[1]

41. Detail of door of catalogue number 12 showing the type of panel found on the latest kasten from the Elting-Beekman shops. Note the continued use of an applied bolection molding with a 17th-century, Dutch-style, ovolo-and-bead profile.

At first glance this kast appears virtually identical to catalogue number 11, which was produced in the Elting-Beekman shops during the first third of the eighteenth century. But closer examination reveals subtle differences in the design of the door panels, front feet, cornice profile, and applied glyphs on the front stiles, which indicate that this example belongs to a later generation of kasten turned out by these shops. In later works like this the door panels are of a very simple fielded design that no longer attempts the dramatic interplay of wide projecting bevels and recessed central fields found in earlier kasten (fig. 24, c). While the ball front feet retain a mound at the top, the mound does not appear to swell up and out of the ball with Baroque dynamism as it does in catalogue number 11; instead it sits awkwardly atop the ball, masking the original intent of the design. The cornice on this late piece is somewhat reduced in scale and lacks the small ovolo profile which is found just below the large upper cyma recta on the earlier designs. Finally, the profile of the applied glyphs no longer comes out of a Mannerist vocabulary; with its central fillet flanked by ovolos, it could easily have been formed by an eighteenth-century window-sash molding plane.

An applied rectangular panel is missing from the center of the drawer. The drawer pulls are modern replacements, as are the left side of the cornice and one of the front feet. As with many Ulster County kasten, on which applied moldings were attached with glue alone, a number of the horizontal moldings have been lost or replaced.

1. A genealogy of the Hasbrouck family is given in Ralph Lefevre and Esther M. Oliver, *History of New Paltz, New York, and Its Old Families from 1678–1820*, 2nd ed. (Albany, 1909).

13. Kast. Ulster County, New York

1740–70

Cherry and pine

H. 77 in. (195.6 cm); O.W. 72 in. (182.9 cm); O.D. 25 7/8 in. (65.7 cm)

Private collection

◆

American kasten with original finishes are rare; only this kast and catalogue numbers 9 and 15 have the thin texture and satinlike sheen that result from two hundred years of oxidation with an occasional waxing. A representative example of the Ulster County style, this kast nonetheless has several design features that differentiate it from products of the dominant Elting-Beekman shop tradition. Most noticeable is the design of the front feet, which are turned in a true ball shape. This profile is found on some Dutch kasten but is unique among American examples. The dovetailed drawer does not run on channels cut into the drawer sides but directly on its thick bottom boards, which are simply butted and nailed to the bottom of the drawer's sides. Lastly, the backboards run horizontally rather than vertically as on all other Ulster County kasten.

For many years the kast belonged to the Lounsbery family, who probably were its original owners. Richard Lounsbery, born about 1700, was the first with that name to settle in Ulster County, moving from New York City to Marbletown in 1725.[1] Subsequent generations prospered in the area. Originally of Welsh descent, the Lounsberys married into local Dutch families, joined the Dutch Reformed Church, and in the second and third generations even adopted the Dutch first name Ritzert instead of Richard. In 1819 Richard's direct descendant, John Lounsbery, purchased a large Georgian-style stone house built in 1771–72 by Cornelius E. Wynkoop.[2] The kast stood in its entrance hall for over 150 years.

Since this kast's unique structural features suggest that it was made outside the dominant shop tradition of Kingston, and since the Lounsbery family had strong ties to the Marbletown area, it seems probable that the maker of the piece was a local Marbletown craftsman. The paneling in the interiors of several houses built in the 1770s demonstrates that talented woodworkers lived in the area.

---

1. A brief genealogy of the Lounsbery family can be found in William Lounsbery, *Three Score and Eleven* (Kingston, N.Y., 1904).

2. Reynolds, *Dutch Houses in the Hudson Valley*, pp. 236–37, pl. 104.

14. Kast. Probably Hempstead, Long Island

1750–70

Cherry and pine

H. 74 in. (188 cm); O.W. 67 1/8 in. (170.5 cm); O.D. 22 1/4 in. (56.5 cm)

Collection of Mrs. Daniel J. Creem

◆

A large group of kasten exists with family histories from the area of Queens and western Nassau counties on Long Island. The constructional details and molding profiles of these kasten set them apart from the more purely Dutch pieces from Kings County and the Hudson River Valley.

This kast probably belonged to Hendrik Onderdonk (1724–1809), a third-generation member of a family that had settled on Long Island in 1672.[1] Onderdonk married Femmetie (Phebe) Tredwell in 1750 and settled at the head of Hempstead Harbor, in what is now the center of Roslyn. He opened a store in 1758, purchased a grist mill and bakehouse, and in 1773 constructed the first paper mill on Long Island. In 1790 George Washington, on a presidential tour, breakfasted at Onderdonk's house (which still stands at the head of Hempstead Harbor), and commented in his diary on his host's entrepreneurial energy.

42. Back of catalogue number 14. Note the full-length, tongue-and-groove backboards and platform feet typical of the one-part construction of Queens County kasten. The cut across the backboards at the height of the waist molding was made later.

The Onderdonk kast was originally constructed in one part (fig. 42) with separate platform feet. At some time the carcase was sawn through at the point where the waist molding is attached. The architrave is not a separate molding but part of the upper carcase, set off by applied, astragal-profile, molded strips. All the molding profiles on this piece, from the flattened curves of the cornice to the distinctive glyphs and narrow waist moldings, are unique to kasten from this part of Long Island.

Although many of the kasten from Queens and western Nassau counties have their stiles either unadorned or ornamented only with applied glyphs, this kast is one of three nearly identical examples with fully articulated Dutch-inspired ornamentation on the stiles.[2] The rectangular panels are wider than those found on examples of more purely Dutch design, however, and are formed by molding strips alone, without an applied center plaque. Conversely, the diamonds on the base are solid applied plaques without applied moldings.

The turning of the platform feet is the most individual feature. The standard proportions are dramatically altered by flattening the ball into a disc shape while the knob at the top and the pad at the bottom are greatly enlarged in scale.

---

1. Attached to the door is a note stating, "This old chest came from the residence of Bishop T. Onderdonk," and also the obituary of his grandson, Alonzo Morris Onderdonk (1862–1938); see Elmer Onderdonk, *Genealogy of the Onderdonk Family in America* (New York, 1910), pp. 31–38.

2. One is at Raynham Hall, Oyster Bay, Long Island (see Failey, *Long Island Is My Nation*, p. 112). Another in a private Long Island collection, purchased from a dealer on the north shore of Queens County, was brought to the attention of the authors by Winterthur Fellow John M. Bacon.

15. Kast. Probably Greenwich, Connecticut

1780–1800

Cherry and poplar

H. 79 in. (200.7 cm); O.W. 67 1/2 in. (171.5 cm); O.D. 22 1/2 in. (57.2 cm)

Collection of Phyllis Arlow and Donald Seeger

◆

Because a number of Long Island families moved across the Sound during the eighteenth century, Connecticut kasten share certain characteristics with mid-Long Island examples, notably one-part construction and platform feet. Kasten made in Connecticut combine a Dutch form with English details. These include the absence of a center stile, doors constructed in the English manner even to the use of butt rather than concealed pivot hinges, and two tiers of drawers. The drawer fronts are detailed with an overlapping ovolo molding as is standard for eighteenth-century New England furniture, rather than with the applied astragal and cavetto molding found on most kasten. The sharp chamfer at the base of the cornice, a detail derived from Dutch Baroque kasten, is absent, and there is no trace of an architrave.

The most idiosyncratic characteristic of kasten made in coastal Connecticut is the construction of the paneling on the front stiles. On either side of the facade are three narrow recessed panels made as openings, then closed by a single long board attached from behind, and finished with applied moldings. The panels thus created are unusual in that they are entirely recessed, with not even their moldings projecting forward from the plane of the stiles.

Nothing is known of the history of this kast, which was discovered in a Federal-period house in Greenwich, Connecticut. It must have been there since before the mid-nineteenth century, when the house was remodeled; at that time the size of the doors was reduced and the kast was sealed in an upstairs bedroom. At least eight similar kasten are known, four with histories in Connecticut in towns as far east as New Haven and as far north as Litchfield.[1]

1. A kast that is similar but has only a single base drawer, found in an 18th-century house in New Haven, was advertised in *Antiques and the Arts Weekly* (Feb. 5, 1988) and was sold at the Litchfield Auction Gallery on February 14, 1988. American clock specialist Ed La Fond acquired a similar example with a southern coastal Connecticut history (letter, Feb. 22, 1988). Peter Eaton provided information about the kast catalogued here and also another example of the type with a Greenwich/Stamford history, currently in a private collection. A closely related kast that has four fielded panels on each door but applied panels and glyphs on the stiles, and which stood in a house in Litchfield at least as far back as 1790, was offered as a gift to the Metropolitan Museum; a photostat is in the files of the Department of American Decorative Arts.

16. Kast. Schraalenburgh (now Bergenfield), New Jersey

Probably by Roelof D. Demarest (1769–1845)

1790–1810

Red gum and yellow poplar; paint added later

H. 79 3/8 in. (201.6 cm); O.W. 73 5/8 in. (187 cm); O.D. 28 1/2 in. (72.4 cm)

Marvill Collection

◆

This well-known kast has been written about and illustrated several times because it is the only known American kast signed by its maker.[1] Written in chalk inside the cupboard top is the inscription, "Made by Roelof Demarest March 17–." Two Roelof Demarests were born in Schraalenburgh in Bergen County, New Jersey. One, Roelof S. Demarest (1756–1814), lived in Bergen County throughout his life; his occupation is unknown. The other, Roelof D. Demarest (1769–1845), is listed as a carpenter in New York City directories, which put him at several addresses during the years 1797–1815. If Roelof D. made this kast he may have done so when he was still living in Bergen County, probably serving an apprenticeship in a local shop. Or he may have been a journeyman carpenter who boarded in New York City residences, working on a job whenever one could be obtained, while still maintaining a business in Bergen County, where he would have built kasten to satisfy conservative local tastes, perhaps even into the early 1800s. Having worked in New York City, Demarest might be responsible for some of the stylish Neoclassical features that are found grafted onto the traditional kast form in Bergen County, including inverted corners in door panels (fig. 26) or the inlaid paterae used in the doors of some examples.[2]

43. Kast, Bergen County, New Jersey, 1790–1810. Red gum, H. 78 in. (198.1 cm). Munson-Williams-Proctor Institute, Museum of Art, Utica, New York. This kast, which is practically identical to catalogue number 16 except for the compass inlays in its doors and its unpainted surface, can also be attributed to the shop of Roelof Demarest.

As a house carpenter Demarest may have taken on the building of kasten because they were part of the architectural interiors of Bergen County homes. Unique to this piece and several other Bergen County kasten is the small bead-and-quirk molding used on the back feet (fig. 25). Demarest also used this molding on three unseen boards on top of the cornice of this kast; it is a profile usually found on door and window architraves in architecture of the Federal period, and its use may indicate that he was first and foremost a house carpenter.

This kast was discovered in an upstairs bedroom of the Isaac Perry house in Pearl River, New York, close by the border of Bergen County, New Jersey. A second kast, probably by a different maker, which is painted in a nearly identical decorative scheme, was in a second upstairs bedroom (fig. 1). It seems likely that in 1830, when the house was greatly expanded, both kasten were given a "fancy" painted treatment with grained, burled, and gilt effects to bring them into decorative harmony with the rest of the interior furnishings.[3]

---

1. Wendy A. Cooper, *In Praise of America* (New York, 1980), p. 225; Joyce Geary Volk, "The Dutch Kast and the American Kas," in *New World Dutch Studies*, pp. 107–17; Blackburn and Piwonka, *Remembrance of Patria*, pp. 262–63.

2. The authors would like to thank Bernard and S. Dean Levy and Mr. Seton Shanley for bringing the kasten with inlaid paterae to their attention.

3. Information on the kasten in the Isaac Perry house was provided by Bernard and S. Dean Levy. The house is illustrated and its changes chronicled in Rosalie Fellows Bailey, *Pre-Revolutionary Dutch Houses and Families in Northern New Jersey and Southern New York* (New York, 1936), p. 203, pl. 56. The second kast found in the Perry house is now owned by the Minneapolis Institute of Arts. Its nearly identically painted surface underwent conservation treatment in 1981 which revealed that the gilding contained a copper alloy, a component of the bronze powders which were usually used to create gilt effects in "fancy" chair painting of the early 19th century (information from accession file 81.3, Minneapolis Institute of Arts).

17. Kast. Probably Ulster County, New York

1730–70

Maple, painted

H. 69 1/2 in. (176.5 cm); O.W. 60 in. (152.4 cm); O.D. 22 in. (55.9 cm)

Collection of William E. Lohrman, New Paltz, New York

◆

The smaller, simpler kast without a base drawer is an important variant of the American Baroque kast form. Surviving examples date from the 1690s to the 1770s or later. Most of them have histories in the central and upper Hudson River Valley; they were probably a less expensive alternative to the Baroque kast made for farmers in the area. The Dutch term *kasje*, or little cupboard, occasionally appears in eighteenth-century New York inventories, and may refer to a kast of this modest scale and price.

A kast of this type usually has two doors, a simple cornice molding, and feet cut directly from the boards that make up the cupboard, often, as here, imitating in shape the turned ball feet of more elaborate examples. Its interior is divided by shelves, as are those of larger kasten, and like them it was used for storage of linens and clothing. Such kasten are generally built of local hardwood (although pine is also used) and frequently are painted. This kast was given at least two coats of blue-gray paint, a popular color in the Hudson River Valley throughout the eighteenth century. Among these simpler kasten the best-known group are those made of yellow poplar or pine and painted with decorations in grisaille (see cat. no. 5).

The placement of four fields on each door of this kast may derive from the design of earlier American examples like the rare oak kast, catalogue number 3. The applied base molding on the kast pictured here is very much like the waist molding on Baroque examples with a drawer in the base. Even the unusual molding profile on the stiles falls comfortably within the conservative mainstream tradition of Ulster County.

Although this kast is said to have come from the Rumpf house, built in Hyde Park, Dutchess County, in the early nineteenth century, its history of ownership is unknown. It displays a particular construction detail—splined corners on the cornice—found only on Ulster County kasten. The fact that a kast nearly identical to this one still stands in a house in New Paltz reinforces its attribution to an Ulster County maker. The profiles on the cornices of both kasten are very close to that on an unattached cornice molding found in the 1712 Jean Hasbrouck house, also in New Paltz.[1]

Another kast, found in Dutchess County, is similar to catalogue number 17 but also different in important ways, and may reflect English influences (fig. 44). Its cornice does not have a corner spline. Small ovolo moldings are worked on the door frames, and the panels are topped with semicircular crests, a motif found in Georgian architecture in Connecticut and occasionally along the eastern side of the Hudson in New York.[2]

44. Kast, probably Dutchess County, New York, 1740–80. Pine, painted green over brick red, H. 68 in. (172.7 cm). Courtesy, Henry Francis du Pont Winterthur Museum

1. Historic American Buildings Survey, Library of Congress, ref. no. Ulster County (56).

2. For Connecticut examples see J. Frederick Kelly, *The Early Domestic Architecture of Connecticut* (New Haven, 1924), fig. 173, pl. 62; for New York examples see Harold D. Eberlein and Cortlandt V. D. Hubbard, *Historic Houses of the Hudson Valley* (New York, 1942), pls. 35, 36.

18. Toy Kast. Kingston, New York

1785–1840

Yellow poplar, sycamore, and pine

H. 9 in. (22.9 cm); O.W. 9 1/2 in. (24.1 cm); O.D. 4 in. (10.2 cm)

New York State Office of Parks, Recreation and Historic Preservation, Senate House State Historic Site

◆

This toy kast contains most of the recognizable characteristics of full-scale kasten, particularly painted kasten (see cat. no. 5), with its extended cornice, central door, large base molding, and turned front feet combined with board rear feet. It retains its original painted decoration, which includes two popular motifs, a tulip on the door and a rose on the cornice. The construction is relatively crude, with wire fasteners used in place of nails or pegs.

The kast was one of a number of pieces of toy furniture, among them a Dutch style *klaptafel* or folding table, that were given to the Senate House in 1892 from the estate of Catherine Vanderlyn (1825–1892). The kast was thought to be old in 1906, when it was illustrated and described as an "old relic" in the *Ulster County Probate Records*.[1] Several members of the artistic Vanderlyn family of Kingston could have constructed and painted this kast, including Catherine Vanderlyn's father Nicholas (1773–1849), a house and coach painter. But a more intriguing candidate is her uncle, the artist John Vanderlyn (1775–1852), who "when a lad . . . displayed great ingenuity in contrivance and manual de[x]terity in execution, constructing toy boxes, carriages and other devices in wood."[2]

1. Gustave Anjou, *Ulster County, New York Probate Records*, 2 vols. (New York, 1906), frontispiece.

2. Robert Gosman, "Biographical Sketch of John Vanderlyn, Artist," reprinted in Louise Hunt Averill, "John Vanderlyn, American Painter (1775–1852)" (Ph.D. diss., Yale University, 1949), p. 298.

19. Spoon Board. Bergen County, New Jersey

Eighteenth century

Yellow poplar

H. 24 in. (61 cm); W. 8 in. (20.3 cm)

Bergen County Historical Society

◆

The carved image of a kast on the crest of this spoon board is an important piece of documentation that records one way the top of an American kast was decorated. Two large ceramic bowls are placed at either end, and a flowerpot with a stylized plant stands in the middle.

Spoon boards, in Dutch-American dialect *lepel borties*, were popular household items in both the Netherlands and the New York area, particularly the Hackensack River Valley of Bergen County, New Jersey.[1] At least sixty American examples are known, all about the same size and with slots for twelve spoons, but only one other depicts a kast on the crest. It is now in the Wallace Nutting Collection at the Wadsworth Atheneum, Hartford, Connecticut.[2]

Usually the decoration on spoon boards is restricted to carved names or initials, dates, and abstract ornament. Known American examples range in date from 1704 to 1803, and are traditionally thought to have been engagement or marriage gifts.

1. Betty Schmelz et al., *The Tree of Life, Selections from Bergen County Folk Art* (River Edge, N.J., 1983), pp. 4–5.

2. Wallace Nutting, "Carved Spoon Racks," *Antiques* 7 (June 1925), pp. 312–15; idem, *Furniture Treasury* (Framingham, Mass., 1928), fig. 4985.

45. Detail of catalogue number 19 showing crest

APPENDIX A

Three-Part American Baroque Kast

With separate cornice, cupboard section, and base

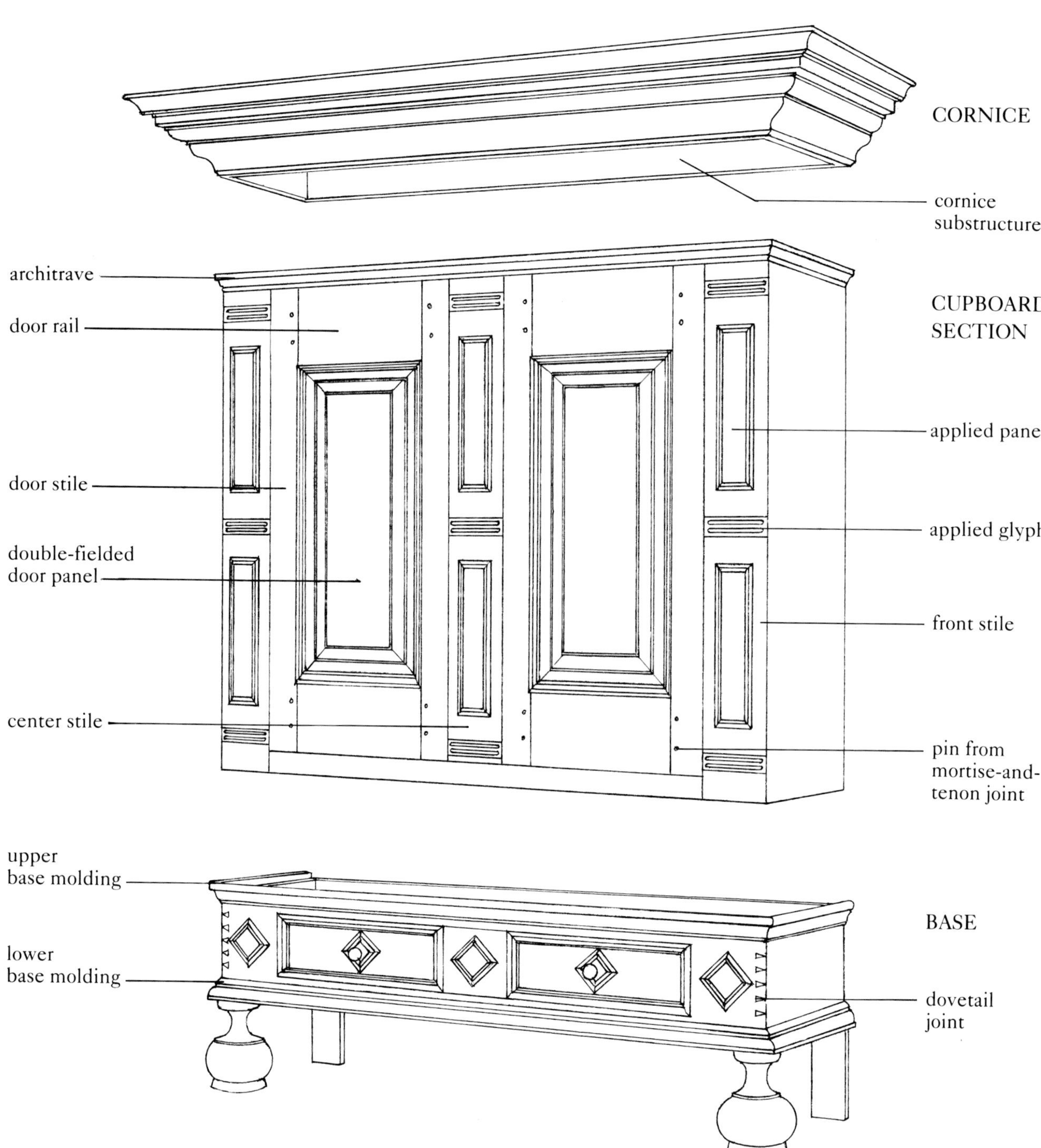

APPENDIX B

Seventeenth-Century Cornices

(true size)

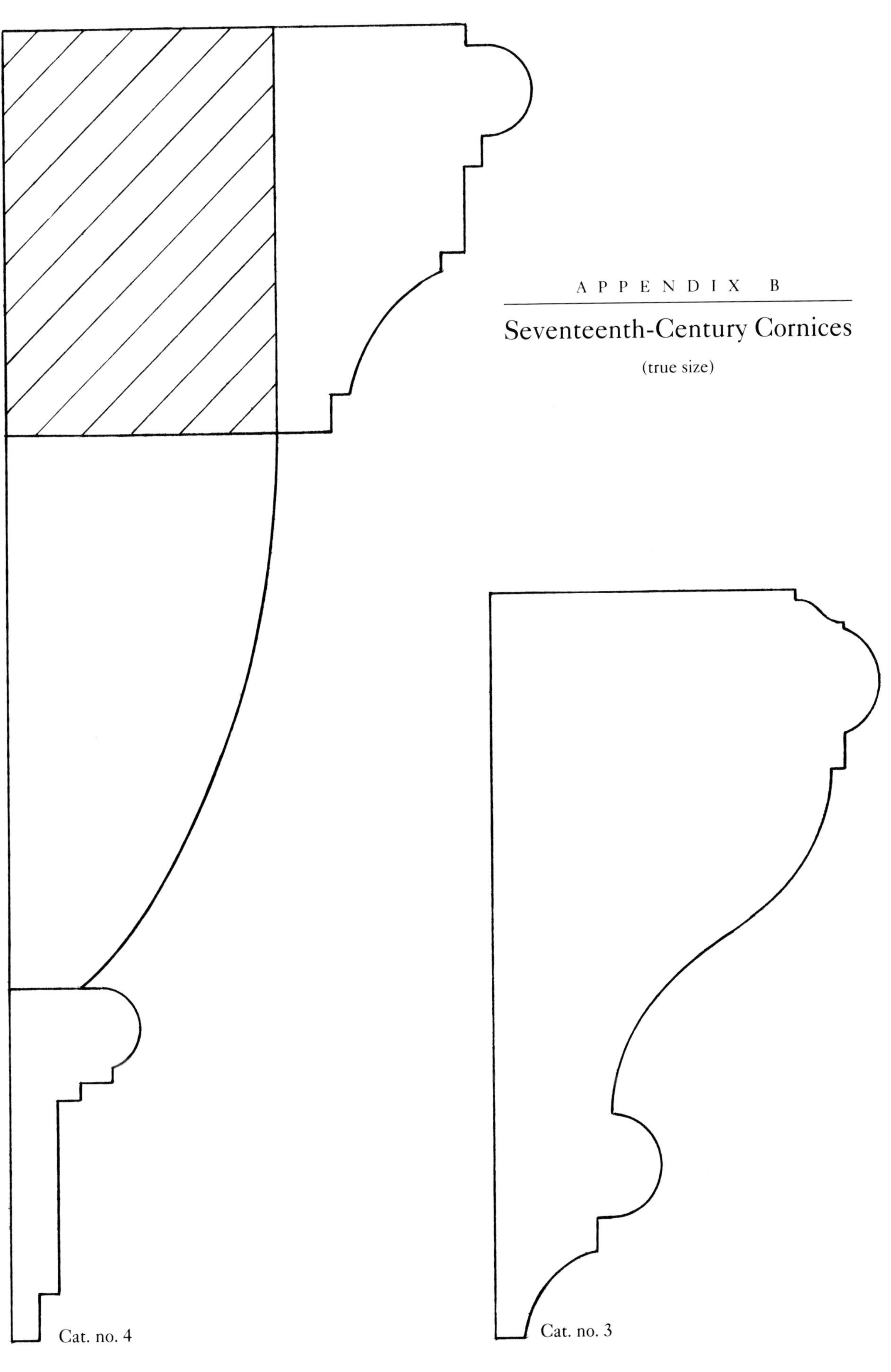

APPENDIX C

Eighteenth-Century Cornices

(true size)

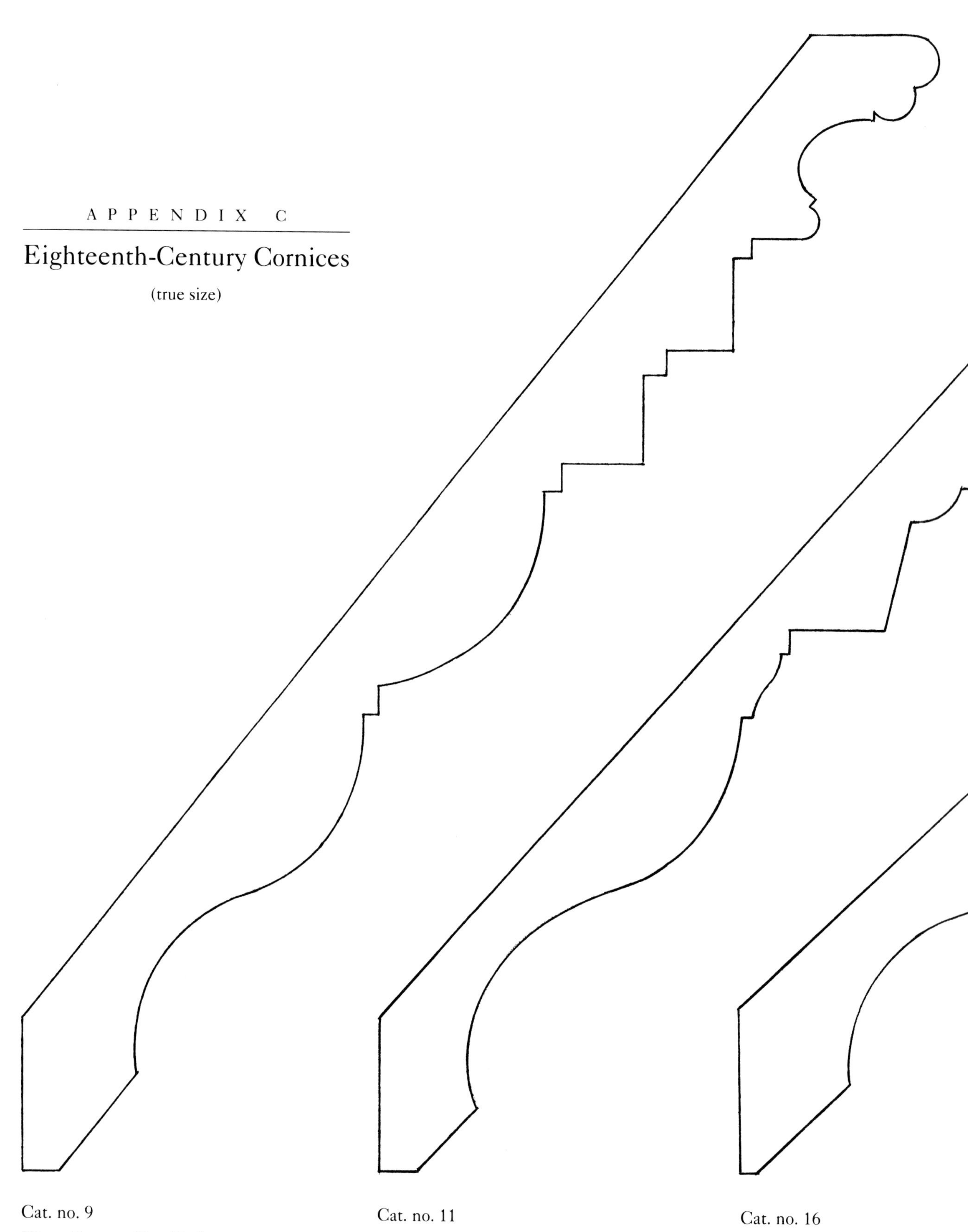

Cat. no. 9
Kings County, New York

Cat. no. 11
Ulster County, New York

Cat. no. 16
Bergen County, New Jersey

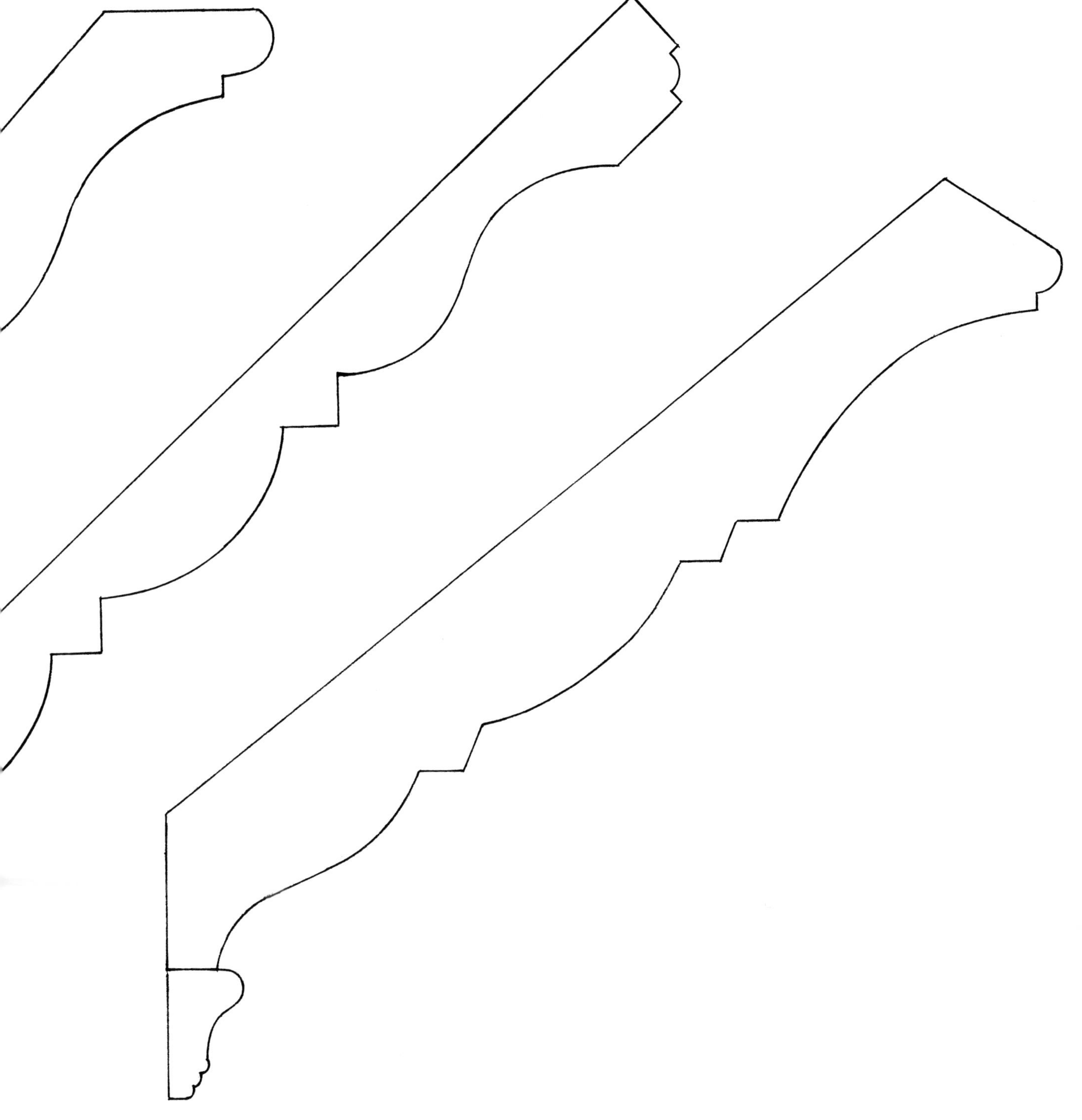

Cat. no. 14
Queens County, New York

APPENDIX D

Upper and Lower Base Moldings

(true size)

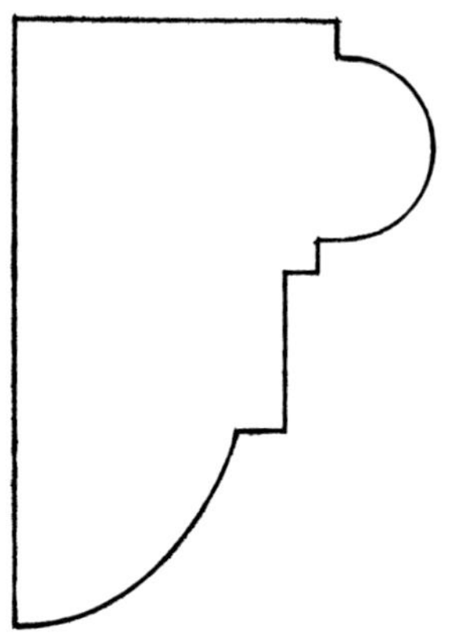

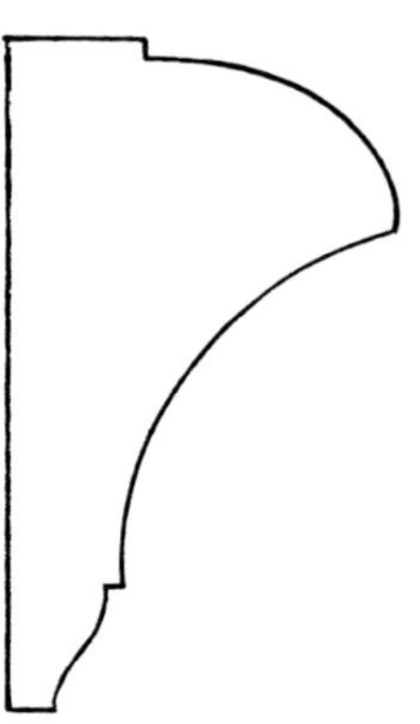

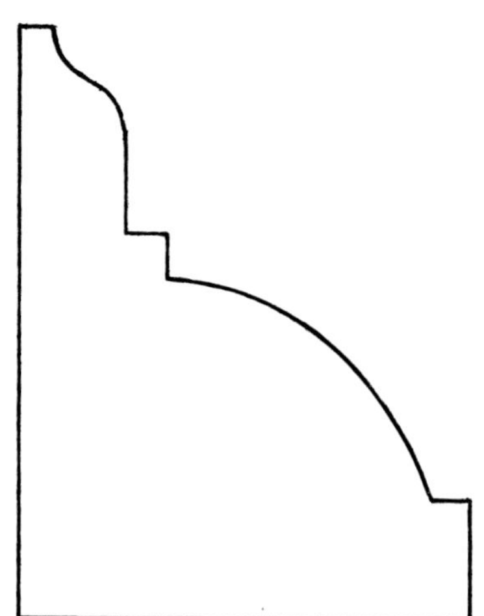

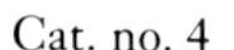

Cat. no. 4

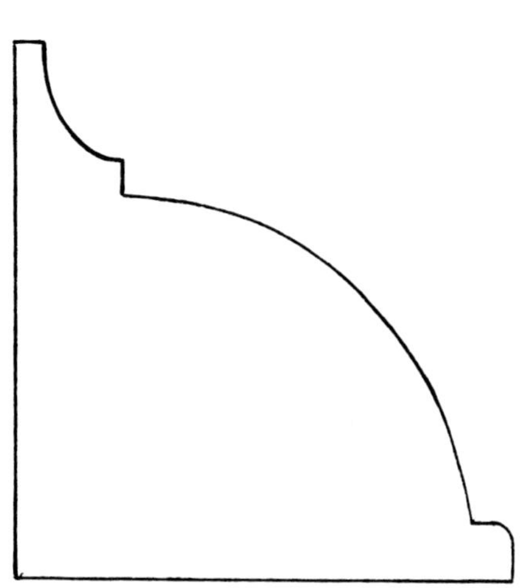

Cat. no. 6

Cat. no

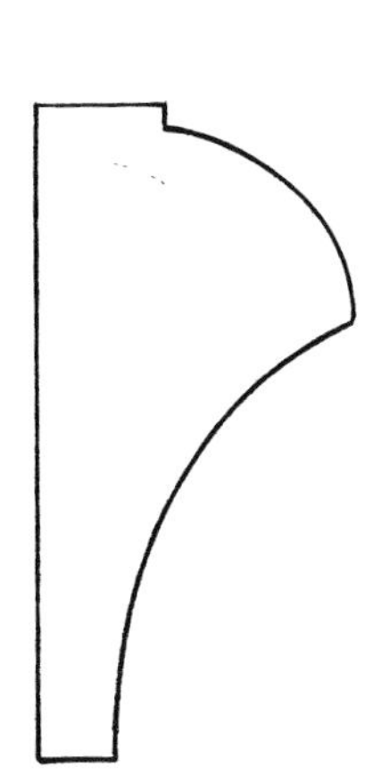

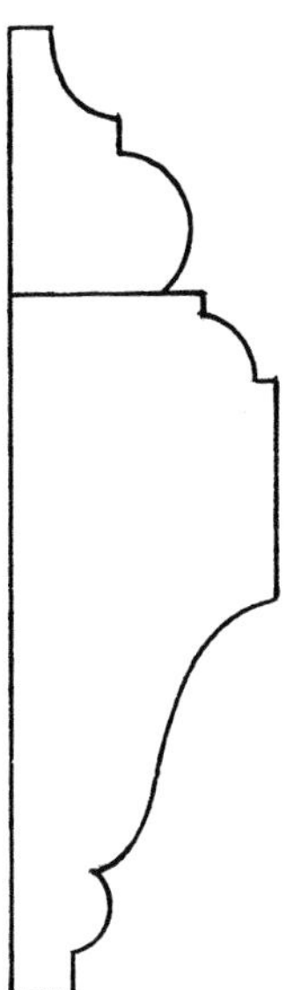

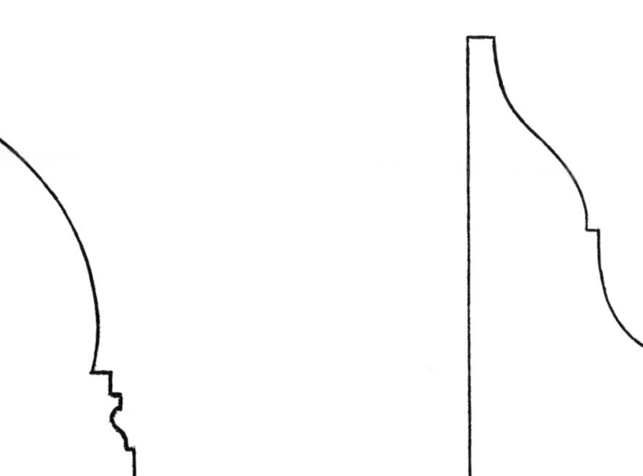

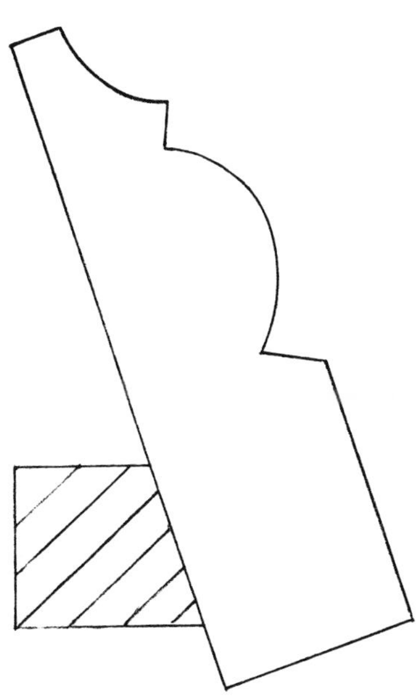

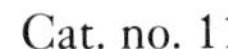

Cat. no. 11

Cat. no. 16

Glossary

◆

Architrave The lowermost of the three divisions of an entablature.

Astragal A small half-round molding; same as bead.

Batten A horizontal wood strip fastened to the back of one or more vertical planks.

Bead Same as astragal.

Bevel An oblique or slanting surface.

Bolection molding An applied molding which surrounds a panel and extends over part of the surrounding framing members.

Book-matched panels Two panels, sawn from the same board and having an identical grain pattern, which are positioned to mirror one another like the pages of an open book.

Butt hinge A common hinge made of two rectangular sections that fit into recesses in the door and the surrounding frame.

Carcase The box-like structure which provides the basic form of a cupboard, cabinet, or chest.

Case piece A general term for a cupboard, cabinet, chest, or any other piece of furniture designed for storage.

Cavetto or cove A molding with a single concave profile, usually a quarter round.

Chamfer A surface produced by cutting away a right-angled corner.

Compass inlay An ornamental device with pointed elements arranged in a circle, reminiscent of the face of a compass.

Cornice The projecting moldings comprising the uppermost division in an entablature.

Cyma recta A double curve molding of which the upper part is concave, the lower part convex.

Cyma reversa A double curve molding, the reverse of the cyma recta, whose upper part is convex and lower part concave.

Dovetail A flaring tenon cut in the shape of a truncated triangle which interlocks with a notch of the same shape.

Double-fielded panel A panel with a smaller field superimposed on a larger one.

Entablature The horizontal area supported by classical columns, consisting of three elements: cornice, frieze, and architrave.

Escutcheon A decorative plate which fits over a keyhole.

Fascia A flat band in a composite molding.

Fielded panel A panel with four beveled sides that surround a flat central surface, or field.

Fillet A small fascia.

Framed Joined.

Frieze The central section of an entablature, between the cornice and the architrave.

Glyph A short straight vertical ornament cut into a frieze of the Doric order. Later the glyph was used as an applied ornament in relief, freely positioned either vertically or horizontally.

Grisaille Painting in monochrome, usually employing shades of gray.

Joined Constructed of horizontal and vertical parts secured by mortise-and-tenon joints.

Kussenkast The Dutch term used in the nineteenth and twentieth centuries for a kast with heavily built-up door panels that project beyond the surface of the door frames.

Miter joint A joint in which two perpendicular parts meet at a 45-degree angle.

Mortise and tenon A joint with a projecting tongue (tenon) that fits into a cavity (mortise).

Muntin A strip separating panes of glass in a window frame.

Ogee A cyma (double curve) molding.

Ovolo A convex, quarter round molding.

Patera A circular or oval ornament used in neoclassical architecture and decoration.

Perimeter molding A molding attached to the face of a door around its outermost edges.

Plinth The block-like element at the base of a column.

Post and lintel A system of architectural construction using upright supports (posts) and horizontal beams (lintels) rather than arches and vaults.

Proud In higher relief than the surrounding surface.

Quirk A narrow groove, square or v-shaped in section.

Rail A horizontal framing member.

Rebate or rabbet A right-angle cut along the edge of a board or framing member.

Reeding Two or more small half-round moldings (beads) set in parallel lines.

Riven Split.

Sash plane A plane used to form window muntins.

Stile A vertical framing member.

Tongue-and-groove joint A joint in which a continuous tenon (the tongue), worked on the edge of one plank, fits into a continuous groove on the edge of another.

Waist molding The upper molding of the base. It separates the cupboard section from the base section.

Waved molding A molding with an undulating pattern, used in Germany and the Netherlands in the seventeenth century, and sometimes called "ripple molding" in the nineteenth century.

Selected Bibliography

◆

Blackburn, Roderic H., and Ruth Piwonka. *Remembrance of Patria: Dutch Arts and Culture in Colonial America, 1609–1776*. Exh. cat. Albany: Albany Institute of History and Art, 1988.

Failey, Dean F. *Long Island Is My Nation: The Decorative Arts & Craftsmen, 1640–1830*. Setauket, New York: Society for the Preservation of Long Island Antiquities, 1976.

Jervis, Simon. *Printed Furniture Designs Before 1650*. [Leeds]: Furniture History Society, 1974.

de Jonge, C. H., and W. Vogelsang. *Holländische Möbel und Raumkunst von 1650–1780*. Stuttgart: Julius Hoffmann, 1922.

Lunsingh Scheurleer, T. H. *Catalogus van meubelen en betimmeringen*. Amsterdam: Rijksmuseum, 1952.

———. "The Dutch and Their Homes in the Seventeenth Century." In *Arts of the Anglo-American Community in the Seventeenth Century*, edited by Ian M. G. Quimby, pp. 13–42. Charlottesville: University Press of Virginia, 1975.

———. "The Low Countries." In *World Furniture: An Illustrated History*, edited by Helena Hayward, pp. 53–56, 72–75. New York: McGraw-Hill, 1965.

New World Dutch Studies: Dutch Arts and Culture in Colonial America, 1609–1776, edited by Roderic H. Blackburn and Nancy A. Kelley. Albany: Albany Institute of History and Art, 1987.

O'Donnell, Patricia Chapin. "Grisaille Decorated *Kasten* of New York." *Antiques* 117 (May 1980), pp. 1108–11.

Schama, Simon. *The Embarrassment of Riches: An Interpretation of Dutch Culture in the Golden Age*. Berkeley and Los Angeles: University of California Press, 1988.

Singleton, Esther. *Dutch New York*. New York: Dodd, Mead and Company, 1909.

———. *The Furniture of Our Forefathers*. New York: Doubleday, Page and Company, 1900.

Sluyterman, K. *Huisraad en binnenhuis in Nederland in vroegere eeuwen*. The Hague: Martinus Nijhoff, 1918.

Acknowledgments

◆

Many individuals and many institutions have assisted us in the preparation of this exhibition and publication, and to all of them we offer our heartfelt thanks. We would like to express special gratitude to those who provided financial support and to the lenders to the exhibition, many of whom kindly allowed us to borrow kasten from their homes.

We are indebted to many members of the Metropolitan Museum's American Wing for their support, chief among them John K. Howat, The Lawrence A. Fleischman Chairman of the Departments of American Art. The departmental staff, in particular Emely Bramson, Ellin Rosenzweig, and Seraphine Wu, were generous with their time. Special thanks are in order for departmental technicians Don Templeton, Gary Burnett, Edward DiFarnecio, and Sean Farrell, who bore up under weighty circumstances. Morrison Heckscher, Curator of American Decorative Arts, was especially encouraging and steadfast in his support from the project's inception, and we are most grateful to him.

Invaluable assistance was provided by people in several other departments of the Museum. We especially want to thank Antoine Wilmering of Objects Conservation for taking such great interest in this project. He, Rudy Colban, Keith Bakker, and John Canonico gave careful and sympathetic treatment to the kasten in need of their attention. In addition we gratefully acknowledge the help and cooperation of Danielle Grosheide, Clare Le Corbeiller, Jessie McNab, Colta Ives, Laurence Kanter, Walter Liedtke, Nina Maruca, Sarah McGregor, and Suzanne Valenstein.

To the many individuals who have aided us through the years in our research on kasten and in the preparation of the exhibition go our thanks and appreciation: Robert S. Alexander, Dale Bennett, Anne Bienstock, Roderic Blackburn, Meg Bleecker, Liz Caffrey, Ann Cassidy, Sarah Clark, Marguerite D'Aprile-Smith, Ulysses Dietz, Peter Eaton, Judy Estes, Michael Ettema, Robert Eurich, Dean Failey, Maxine Friedman, Dr. Roger Gerry, Richard Goring, Nina Gray, Barry Harwood, John Hays, Daniel Hopping, Tom Hughes, Pat Jacques, Fred Johnston, Leigh Jones, Ann Kaufman, Nancy Kelley, Ann Kohls, Ed La Fond, Greg Landry, Allison Ledes, Bernard Levy, Dean Levy, Bill Lohrman, Clare McDonald, Celia McGee, Helen McLallen, Milo Naeve, Janet O'Dence, Liz and Dave Quakenbush, Thoma Robertson, Bob Slater, Kevin Stayton, Jerry Thompson, Jane Townsend, Robert Trent, Deborah Waters, Nancy Waters, Rebecca Watrous, Peter Wisbey, and Kevin Wright. We are also grateful to the staff of the New York State Historical Association library.

Special thanks go to our colleagues abroad: Bill Cotton, Alma Ruempol, T. H. Lunsingh Scheurleer, Reinier Baarsen, Henk Zantkuyl, and particularly Jaap Schipper, who through the years has been exceedingly generous with his help. In addition we would like to thank J. B. van Heek and the Edwina van Heek Foundation, Enschede, the Netherlands.

Finally, this catalogue would never have become a reality without the guidance and able assistance of Barbara Burn and the highly professional staff of the Editorial Department, including the director of the book's production, Susan Chun, and the designer, Margaret Davis. To Ruth Kozodoy, who skillfully and patiently edited the book, the authors are most grateful.

Peter M. Kenny
Frances Gruber Safford
Gilbert T. Vincent